THE KAMOGAWA
FOOD DETECTIVES

Hisashi Kashiwai was born in 1952 and was raised in Kyoto. He graduated from Osaka Dental University. After graduating, he returned to Kyoto and worked as a dentist. He has written extensively about his native city and has collaborated on TV programmes and magazines.

Jesse Kirkwood is a literary translator working from Japanese into English. The recipient of the 2020 Harvill Secker Young Translators' Prize, his translations include *The Kamogawa Food Detectives* by Hisashi Kashiwai, *Tokyo Express* by Seicho Matsumoto and *A Perfect Day to Be Alone* by Nanae Aoyama.

The Kamogawa
Food Detectives

HISASHI KASHIWAI

Translated from the Japanese by Jesse Kirkwood

PAN BOOKS

First published in the UK 2023 by Mantle

This paperback edition first published 2024 by Pan Books
an imprint of Pan Macmillan
The Smithson, 6 Briset Street, London EC1M 5NR
EU representative: Macmillan Publishers Ireland Ltd, 1st Floor,
The Liffey Trust Centre, 117–126 Sheriff Street Upper,
Dublin 1, D01 YC43
Associated companies throughout the world
www.panmacmillan.com

ISBN 978-1-0350-0959-6

Originally published in Japan as *Kamogawashokudo* by Shogakukan in 2013.
Japanese/English translation rights arranged with Shogakukan
through Emily Publishing Company, Ltd.
and Casanovas & Lynch Literary Agency S.L.

1 3 5 7 9 8 6 4 2

A CIP catalogue record for this book is available from the British Library.

Typeset in Sabon by Jouve (UK), Milton Keynes
Printed and bound by CPI Group (UK) Ltd, Croydon, CR0 4YY

CONTENTS

Chapter 1:
Nabeyaki-Udon

1

Walking away from Higashi Honganji temple, Hideji Kuboy-ama instinctively turned up the collar on his trench coat.

Dead leaves swirled in the chilly air. That must be the famous Mount Hiei wind, he thought to himself, knitting his brows as he waited for the signal to change.

It was just like people said: in Kyoto, the cold cuts to the bone. In midwinter, freezing air rushes down from the mountains that surround the city on three sides. In Kobe, where Hideji had been born and raised, the winds that blew down from Mount Rokko were formidable too. But here, the quality of the cold was somehow different. As he made his way down Shomen-dori, he cast his gaze towards the snow-capped peaks of the Higashiyama mountains in the distance.

Hideji stopped a postman sitting astride a red scooter and asked for directions. 'Excuse me. I'm looking for a restaurant round here. The Kamogawa Diner, I think it's called.'

'If it's Mr Kamogawa you're after, his is the second building after that corner,' replied the postman in an extremely matter-of-fact tone, pointing down the right-hand side of the street.

Hideji crossed the street and stood in front of the two-storey structure. It didn't look much like a restaurant, though traces of a former sign and a display window remained. Two squares of white paint had been scruffily applied to the exterior wall. However, it had none of the gloominess of a vacant building, instead radiating a human warmth that suggested it was still very much a working restaurant. While its appearance might have been off-putting to the average tourist, the smells drifting out were enticing, and from inside came the sound of cheerful banter.

'This place has Nagare written all over it,' muttered Hideji, casting his mind back to the days he'd spent with Nagare Kamogawa, his former colleague. The two of them had both moved on to other things now. Despite being Hideji's junior, Nagare had been the first to quit the police.

He looked up at the restaurant, then opened the sliding aluminium door.

'Welcome to – oh! If it isn't Hideji!' Koishi Kamogawa, a round tray in her hands, froze with surprise. Koishi was

Nagare's only daughter, and Hideji had known her since she was a baby.

'Koishi! Well, aren't you all grown up,' said Hideji, removing his coat.

'Hideji? Is that you?' called Nagare as he emerged from the kitchen in his white apron.

'So this *is* your place, after all,' said Hideji, grinning broadly at Nagare.

'I can't believe you found us. Please, take a seat. Sorry the place isn't much to look at.' Nagare wiped down the red cushion of one of the chairs.

'I guess I haven't lost my intuition yet,' said Hideji, blowing into his numb hands to warm them as he sat down.

'How many years has it been, you reckon?' asked Nagare as he removed his chef's hat.

'I suppose the last time was your wife's funeral.'

'You were a real help that day,' said Nagare, bowing in gratitude. Koishi followed suit.

'I don't suppose you could rustle something up for me? I'm ravenous,' said Hideji, glancing sideways at a young man who was shovelling down a bowl of katsudon.

'I usually ask first-time customers to leave it up to the chef,' said Nagare.

'Sounds good to me,' said Hideji, meeting Nagare's gaze.

'Coming right up, then. Just give me a moment,' said Nagare, donning his hat again as he turned away.

'Oh – and no mackerel, please!' said Hideji, before taking a sip of his tea.

'Don't worry – I remember. We've known each other long enough!' replied Nagare over his shoulder.

Hideji looked around the restaurant. Apart from the young man, the five counter seats by the kitchen were unoccupied. There was no one else sitting at the four tables either, and nothing resembling a menu in sight. The clock on the wall showed ten past one.

'Koishi, can I get some tea?' said the man eating katsu-don, setting his now-empty bowl down on the counter.

'You shouldn't wolf your food down like that, Hiroshi. It's bad for your digestion,' said Koishi, pouring tea from a small Kiyomizu-ware teapot. Meanwhile, Nagare brought out Hideji's food on a tray.

'Looks like quite the feast!' said Hideji, his eyes widening.

'Not really. They call it "Kyoto comfort food" these days, but in the past no one would have dreamed of charging people money for simple fare like this. Still, I thought it might be the sort of thing you'd enjoy.' Nagare was unloading various dishes and small bowls from the tray, arranging them one by one on the table.

'You're not wrong. Looks like *your* intuition hasn't faded either.'

As Hideji's gaze skipped between the various dishes, Nagare went on:

'Stewed arame and deep-fried tofu. Okara croquettes. Kikuna leaves dressed with sesame and miso. Kurama-style sardine. Hirosu tofu ball in broth. Pork belly simmered in Kyobancha tea. Fresh tofu curd with sour plum paste. Oh, and Koishi's rice-bran-pickled cucumbers. Nothing too extravagant. If anything, the highlights are probably the firmly cooked Goshu rice and the miso soup with ebi-imo taro. Anyway, enjoy the meal. Oh, and make sure you put a good sprinkle of sansho pepper on the soup – it'll warm you right up.'

His eyes gleaming, Hideji nodded along to Nagare's every word.

'Tuck in while it's hot!' urged Koishi. Hideji sprinkled the sansho pepper and picked up the bowl of miso soup. When he sipped it one of the chunks of taro tumbled into his mouth. Chewing on it slowly, he nodded once, twice, and then a third time.

'This miso soup's fantastic. What rich flavours!'

With the thin-rimmed rice bowl in his left hand, his chopsticks danced back and forth between the dishes, reaching towards each in turn. He took a piece of the pork belly, dripping with sauce, and set it on top of the white rice before transporting it to his mouth. As he carefully bit into the meat, a smile began to spread across his face. Next he crunched through the coating of the okara croquette, savouring the soy pulp filling. When he placed the hirosu tofu ball on his tongue, the delicately flavoured broth oozed out, some of it spilling from his mouth. Hideji wiped his chin with the hand holding his chopsticks.

'More rice?' asked Koishi, offering him her tray.

'You know, I haven't eaten this well in quite a while,' said Hideji, placing his depleted rice bowl on the tray.

'Well then, better eat your fill!' said Koishi, hurrying off to the kitchen with the tray.

'Is the food alright?' said Nagare, coming over to the table just as Koishi was leaving.

'More than alright. I'm struggling to believe a mere mortal acquaintance of mine could have put this kind of meal together.'

'Oh, no need for that kind of talk. I'm just an old codger who happens to run a restaurant,' said Nagare, looking humbly at the floor.

'So, Hideji, what are you up to these days?' said Koishi, appearing again with the bowl, now piled high with rice.

'I retired from the force last year. I'm on the board of a security company in Osaka now,' said Hideji, gazing eagerly at the glistening white rice before getting to work with his chopsticks.

'Sounds like they've sorted you out with a nice position. I have to say though – you haven't changed a bit. Still got that sharp look in your eyes!' said Nagare, meeting Hideji's gaze.

'The bitterness of these kikuna leaves works very nicely. A real Kyoto flavour, isn't it.' Hideji positioned the rest of the salad on top of his rice before polishing it off. Then he crunched on one of the pickled cucumbers.

'How about steeping your rice in tea? You could mix it with some of the sardine. Koishi, why don't you pour him some hojicha?'

Taking her cue, Koishi poured the hot tea from a Banko teapot.

'So you call it Kurama-style in Kyoto. Where I'm from, if you simmer something with sansho pepper, that's Arima-style.'

'Must be a case of local pride then. Kurama and Arima are both famous for their sansho, aren't they?'

'You learn something new every day!' said Koishi.

When he had finished the steeped rice, Hideji picked his teeth, then settled back in his chair.

To the right of the counter seating, an indigo curtain hung over the entrance to the kitchen. Whenever Nagare passed through the curtain, Hideji caught a glimpse of a tatami-matted living room alongside the kitchen space, where a grand-looking Buddhist altar was set into the wall.

'Mind if I pay my respects?' asked Hideji, peering past the curtain. Koishi led him to the altar.

'You're looking younger, Hideji!' said Koishi, putting her hands on Hideji's shoulders and taking in his features.

'I hope you're not making fun of me. I've passed the sixty mark, you know.' Hideji kneeled and positioned a stick of incense in front of the altar, then set the cushion to one side.

'Thanks for doing this,' said Nagare, glancing over at the portrait on the altar and lowering his head.

'So, Kikuko watches over you while you work?' Still kneeling on the tatami mat, Hideji relaxed into a less formal pose and looked up at Nagare.

'More like keeps an eye on me,' replied Nagare with a chuckle.

'I never would have thought you'd end up running a restaurant, you know.'

'Actually, I've been meaning to ask since you walked in here. How *did* you find us?' asked Nagare, coming over and sitting by him on the tatami.

'Well, my boss is a bit of a foodie. He likes to read *Gourmet Monthly*, and keeps a stack of back issues in the boardroom. When I saw your advert in the magazine, I put two and two together.'

'Now see, that's why we called you Hideji the Hawk. I can't believe you knew it was my restaurant from a one-line advert like that. There weren't even any contact details! And yet here you are.' Nagare was shaking his head in admiration.

'Knowing you, I'm sure there's a reason, but couldn't you make that advert a little less mysterious? The way it reads at the moment, I'll probably be the only one to ever find you!'

'Oh, that's alright by me. I'd rather not be swamped with customers.'

'You always were a funny one, Nagare.'

'So, hoping we can track down a dish from your past, by any chance?' asked Koishi, studying Hideji as she stood at Nagare's side.

'Yes, I think I might be,' said Hideji, a smile playing about his lips.

'You still living over in Teramachi?' asked Nagare, getting up and walking over to the sink.

'The same old place by Junenji temple. Every morning I walk along the Kamogawa river to Demachiyanagi, then jump on the Keihan line for my commute to the Osaka office. Phew, all this kneeling is tough. At this age, my legs just can't take it!'

Frowning, Hideji slowly raised himself from the tatami and returned to his seat in the restaurant.

'Oh, tell me about it. It's always a struggle when the priest comes over for Kikuko's death day.'

'Good on you for getting a priest in though,' said Hideji. 'I haven't had one over to pray for my wife for years. Bet she's furious.' He took a cigarette from his breast pocket, then glanced at Koishi as if to gauge her reaction.

'Oh, go ahead,' said Koishi, setting an aluminium ashtray on the table.

'Excuse me,' said Hideji, waving his cigarette in the direction of Hiroshi. 'Mind if I have a quick puff?'

'Be my guest,' replied Hiroshi with a grin, before retrieving a cigarette of his own from his bag.

'Don't you think it's time you gave up? It's one thing smoking when you're young, but at our age . . .' said Nagare across the counter.

'I've been hearing that a lot recently,' said Hideji, then took a long drag on his cigarette.

'You have? Wait – don't tell me you've remarried?'

'Actually, that's what brings me here. See, I need your help recreating a certain . . . flavour,' said Hideji, smiling as he stubbed his cigarette out in the ashtray.

'Thanks for the katsudon – it was delicious,' said Hiroshi, slapping a five-hundred-yen coin on the counter and walking out of the restaurant with his cigarette dangling from his mouth. Hideji, following him with his gaze, turned to Koishi.

'That some sweetheart of yours?'

'Oh, Hideji, shush!' said Koishi, blushing as she thumped Hideji on the back. 'He's just one of our regulars. Runs a sushi place around the corner.'

'Hideji, sorry to be so formal, but it's Koishi who runs the detective agency. Could you fill her in on what it is you're looking for? Our office – if you can call it that – is in the back.'

'Got it. Alright then, Koishi, ready when you are,' said Hideji, making as if to get up.

'I'll just be a moment,' said Koishi, removing her apron and hurrying to the back of the kitchen.

'So, Nagare, how long are *you* going to keep this widower thing up?' said Hideji, settling back into his chair.

'Well, it's only been five years, hasn't it? If I marry someone else too soon, Kikuko will come back and haunt me, I just know it,' said Nagare, pouring them some tea.

'Still too early for you, eh? It'll be fifteen years ago this year for me. I figure Chieko will be just about ready to forgive me by now.'

'Has it really been that long? Goes quickly, doesn't it. Feels like just the other the day that she was inviting me around for dinner.'

'She had her foibles, but one thing's for sure – no one could cook like her,' said Hideji with a sigh. There was a moment's silence.

'Well, shall we?' said Nagare, getting to his feet. Hideji followed his lead.

At the other end of the counter to the kitchen entrance was a small door. Nagare opened it to reveal a long, narrow corridor which, it seemed, led to the detective agency's office.

'Are these all your creations?' said Hideji, looking at the

photos of food plastered along the walls as he followed
Nagare down the corridor.

'Not quite all of them, but yes,' replied Nagare over his
shoulder.

'And this . . . ?' Hideji had come to a halt.

'I've been drying red chilli peppers in the back garden.
Trying to do it the way Kikuko used to. Haven't had much
luck, though . . .'

'I remember Chieko drying something or other that way
too. It all seemed like a bit of a faff to me, mind . . .' said
Hideji, walking again.

'Koishi, your client's here,' said Nagare, opening the
door at the end of the corridor.

'Sorry to be a pain, but could you write a few things down
for me?'

Koishi was sitting on a sofa opposite Hideji, on the other
side of a low table.

'Name, age, date of birth, address, occupation . . .
Sheesh, feels like I'm taking out an insurance policy!'
chuckled Hideji, opening up the folding clipboard Koishi
handed him.

'I wouldn't worry too much about the details, seeing as
it's you.'

'Oh, but I'm a former bureaucrat. You won't catch *me* cutting corners!' said Hideji, returning the clipboard.

'Diligent as ever, aren't you,' said Koishi, scanning Hideji's rows of carefully printed characters and sitting up. 'So, what dish are you looking for?'

'Nabeyaki-udon. You know, vegetables and chicken simmered with udon noodles.'

'Any other details?' said Koishi, flipping open her notebook.

'Well, it's the kind my wife used to make.'

'I see. It's been a while since she passed away, hasn't it?'

'Fifteen long years.'

'And you still remember the taste?'

Hideji nodded, then tilted his head to one side as if he'd changed his mind.

'Well, I have a rough idea of the flavour, and the kinds of ingredients she used, but . . .'

'No matter how you try, it never quite tastes the same?'

'Exactly. I see you've got your father's intuition!'

'Hideji, please don't tell me you've remarried and now you're asking your new wife to cook this for you?'

'Would that be so bad?'

'Of course it would. It's a total no-no! Trying to get her to recreate a flavour bound up with memories of your previous wife . . . I mean, really!'

13

'You jump to conclusions just like Nagare too! I wouldn't have the nerve to try something like that. No, all I did was ask if she could try cooking us a nice nabeyaki-udon. Anyway, she's not my wife yet. She works in my office, and she's been married once already, just like me. The two of us get along like a house on fire. She comes over to my place from time to time, cooks us a bite to eat.'

'I see you've really rediscovered your youth. All loved up, are we?' said Koishi, glancing up as she teased him.

'At my age, it's not quite the whirlwind romance you're imagining. It's more about companionship – you know, someone I can share a cup of tea with.' Smiling bashfully, Hideji went on. 'Nami Sugiyama, her name is, but everyone just calls her Nami-chan. She's a little younger than me, but she ranks way above me at the office. She handles all the accounts, and the boss really trusts her. We're a real duo. Trips to the movies, strolls around the temples – just having *fun*, you know.'

'A new lease of life,' said Koishi with a grin.

'She's living on her own over in Yamashina right now, but her family home is up north. Takasaki, in Gunma prefecture. Her mother passed away a couple of months ago, leaving her father on his own. She says she's going to move back there to look after him.'

'On her own, you mean?'

'Well, actually, she asked if I'd go with her,' said Hideji, his facing turning a bright shade of red.

'Congratulations! I mean, that's basically a proposal, isn't it?' said Koishi, clapping her hands in gentle applause.

'My son has given the okay too, so it looks like it's going ahead. The only problem is food. You know, with her being from up north and all . . .' said Hideji, his expression clouding over.

'And that's where the nabeyaki-udon comes in?'

'Now, I don't mean to harp on about Nami, but she really does know how to cook. Not just Japanese food – though you should see the nikujaga stew or the seasoned rice she cooks up! No, when it comes to non-Japanese stuff – curry, say, or hamburger steaks, she puts the pros to shame. Makes her own gyoza and steamed buns, too. I have nothing at all to complain about. It's much better than you'd get in some lousy restaurant! The thing is, though, her nabeyaki-udon just doesn't quite hit the spot. She really tries to make it tasty, you know. But there's a world of difference between hers and the one Chieko used to make. And nabeyaki-udon is my absolute favourite. So you see . . .'

'Got it. Dad'll think of something. You can count on us!' said Koishi, patting her chest confidently.

'Sounds like I'm mainly counting on your dad!' chuckled Hideji.

'Could you give me a few more details? Do you know

what dashi stock Chieko used, or what ingredients she added?' asked Koishi, pen at the ready.

'The dashi tasted like something you'd get at an udon place in Kyoto. I don't think the ingredients were unusual. Chicken, negi onion, sliced kamaboko, dried wheat cake, shiitake mushrooms, prawn tempura and egg. That was all.'

'What about the udon?'

'They weren't those thick Sanuki noodles you see everywhere these days. They were softer than that. You know, sort of . . . squishy.'

'Sounds like she used proper Kyoto udon. Well, I've got a decent idea of the dish now. But, Hideji, you've tried telling Nami all this, haven't you? And yet it still ended up tasting different. This could be a tricky one to solve . . .' Koishi was frowning.

'Maybe it *was* the ingredients that were different. Or the seasoning. I just don't know . . .'

'Didn't Chieko ever say anything? You know – about where she bought the udon, or the other ingredients?'

'Well, I've never been that interested in cooking myself, you see. But . . . there was this one phrase she used to mumble. *Masu, suzu, fuji.* Something like that . . .'

'*Masu, suzu, fuji.* That was it?'

'Yes. Just before she set off to do the shopping, she'd always chant it, like some Buddhist mantra. I can still hear her now.'

'Was there anything else? Something you remember about the flavour, for example?'

'I remember thinking it always tasted a little bitter at the end.'

'Bitter? You mean the dish as a whole?'

'Not exactly. It was more the aftertaste . . . But I might be wrong. I'm probably getting mixed up with something else she used to make.'

'Hard to imagine nabeyaki-udon tasting bitter . . .' said Koishi, thumbing through her notebook.

'If I could just eat it one more time, I'd feel a lot better about going off to live in Takasaki. I'm sure I'll get used to Nami's version once I'm there. When in Rome, and all that . . .'

'Alright then. We're on the case!' said Koishi, snapping her notebook shut.

When Hideji and Koishi returned to the restaurant, Nagare turned the television off with the remote.

'Did the interview go alright?'

'I wish I could say it went swimmingly, but . . .' replied Koishi in an uncertain voice.

'Looks like I've landed you with a tough one. Don't let this case go cold, you hear?' said Hideji, slapping Nagare on the shoulder.

'After all, this is Hideji's chance to enjoy a new lease

of life!' chimed in Koishi. Following Hideji's lead, she thumped Nagare on the back.

'I'll do my absolute best,' said Nagare, his nose wrinkling slightly.

'So, how much do I owe you?' said Hideji, putting on his coat and taking out his wallet.

'Oh, please! You left such a kind offering for my wife, and I haven't given you anything in return. Treating you to a meal is the least I can do . . .'

'Ah, you found that, did you? I thought I hid it under the incense holder.'

'Oh, don't go thinking you can slip something like that past me!' The two men caught each other's eye and laughed.

'Hideji, about your next visit – would two weeks today work?' asked Koishi.

'Two weeks today . . . Yes, that'll be perfect. I'm off work that day.' Hideji opened his diary, licked his pencil, and scribbled down the date.

'You look just like you used to when we went around questioning people,' said Nagare with a smile.

'Old habits die hard, eh?' Hideji slid his diary back into his inner pocket and stepped out into the street. As he did so, a tabby cat scarpered away from the door.

'What's wrong, Drowsy? He won't hurt you!' called Koishi.

'Is that your cat? It wasn't here a moment ago . . .'

'He started hanging around here about five years ago. He's always half asleep, so we call him Drowsy. He has it rough, though – Dad never stops bullying the poor thing!'

'It's hardly bullying. You just can't have a cat running around when you're making food for people.' Nagare whistled, but Drowsy, stretched out on the other side of the road, seemed to be pretending not to hear him.

'Well, I'm counting on you!' said Hideji, and walked off down the street, making his way west.

'Another tough case, then?' said Nagare, glancing at Koishi by his side.

'Shouldn't be too tricky. Hideji knows exactly the dish he's after – he just hasn't managed to recreate it,' replied Koishi, sliding open the door.

'What dish would that be, then?' said Nagare, walking back into the restaurant and taking a seat.

'Nabeyaki-udon,' said Koishi, sitting down opposite him.

'From a particular restaurant?'

'No, the way his wife used to make it,' said Koishi, opening up her notebook on the table.

'Oh. Then it *will* be tricky, trust me. Chieko really knew

her way round the kitchen. It sounds like nostalgia might be the secret ingredient here . . .' said Nagare, flicking through Koishi's notes.

'The ingredients are all pretty standard, right? But Hideji says he just can't get it to taste the same . . .'

'Chieko was a proper Kyoto lady. I can imagine the sort of seasoning she used. And if they lived in Teramachi . . .' Nagare crossed his arms as he racked his brains.

'Did you know Chieko, then?'

'Know her? We were good friends. She even cooked for me a few times.'

'In that case, shouldn't this be an easy one to solve?'

'But I don't remember ever trying her nabeyaki-udon . . .' Nagare scanned Koishi's notes carefully.

'This new girlfriend of his – apparently she's a good ten years or so younger than him! Bet you're jealous.'

'Don't be silly. How many times do I have to tell you: your mother is the only one for me. Anyway, this Nami – she's from Gunma prefecture up north, is that right?' asked Nagare, looking up.

'Yes, I think so. He said her family was from Takasaki.'

'Takasaki, eh . . .' said Nagare pensively.

'Dad, I feel like nabeyaki-udon all of a sudden. How about having it for dinner?'

'Oh yes. And not just tonight, either. It's nabeyaki every night until we crack this one,' said Nagare, without looking up from the notebook.

2

In Kyoto they say the real cold of winter only strikes after Setsubun – the day in early February when, traditionally, people scatter beans out of their front door to ward off evil spirits. As Hideji made his way down Shomen-dori in the dusk, he couldn't help thinking they were right.

From somewhere came the sound of an itinerant tofu seller's horn. Groups of schoolchildren, all shouldering identical leather backpacks, cut right past him as they hurried home. It was as though he'd slipped back in time to another era. Hideji came to a halt in front of the Kamogawa Diner, his long shadow stretching across the pavement.

Drowsy the cat must have remembered him, because he came over and began curling himself around his legs.

'Nagare been bullying you again?' he said, leaning over and stroking the tabby's head, eliciting a soft *miaow*.

'You're early! Hurry on in. It's chilly out there!' said Koishi, sliding open the door and bowing.

'You better let this cat in, or he'll catch cold.'

'I'm pretty sure cats don't catch colds. Anyway, Dad'll flip if he sees him.'

'Koishi! Don't let that cat in here!' shouted Nagare from the kitchen.

'See what I mean?' said Koishi with a wink.

'Still do it every year, do you?' muttered Hideji as he removed his coat.

'Do what?' said Koishi, bringing over a pot of tea.

'The bean-scattering ceremony. Oh, I can just picture it: Nagare out in front, chucking the beans and shouting 'Devils *out*! Fortune *in*!', and you chiming in from behind. Sticking to the old traditions – you two are real Kyotoites, aren't you?'

'But . . . how did you know?' Koishi seemed bewildered.

'There are beans stuck in the sill of your door,' said Hideji, glancing sharply at the entrance.

'Really haven't changed a bit, have you?' said Nagare, looking out from the kitchen in his white apron.

'Sorry I'm early. Just couldn't wait. And at this age I can't stand being in a rush.'

'Thanks for making the time,' said Nagare, bowing slightly from behind the counter.

'I did exactly as you told me. I haven't eaten anything since my usual cafe breakfast, early this morning.' Hideji downed his tea in one gulp, perhaps in an attempt to stave off his hunger.

'Just give me ten minutes,' called Nagare.

'So, things going smoothly with Nami?' asked Koishi as she laid the table. Alongside an indigo-dyed place mat, she set a pair of cedar chopsticks on a holly-shaped chopstick rest. Then she placed a Karatsu-ware bowl in the middle of the table, with a celadon-green spoon on the right.

'Handed in her resignation last week. She's back in Takasaki now. The boss was sad to see her go,' said Hideji, fishing out an evening paper from the magazine rack.

'Bet you've been having to eat out every night.'

'Yes – that or ready meals from the convenience store. Getting a little sick of it, to be honest!' said Hideji, lowering the open newspaper as he laughed.

'Hang in there. You'll be in Takasaki with your sweetheart before you know it,' said Koishi, her eyes sparkling.

'Oh, I don't know about that. Getting a new father-in-law at my age won't be a very sweet experience, I can tell you.'

'I guess that's life, eh?' said Nagare, setting a woven straw pot stand by Hideji's place mat. 'Sometimes you have to take the bitter with the sweet.'

'Ah, here it comes. The moment of truth!' said Hideji, folding up the newspaper and sitting up in his chair.

'Oh, leave the newspaper open. Just like back in the day,' said Nagare as he headed back to the kitchen.

'How did you know I used to do that?' asked Hideji, blinking in surprise.

'I haven't shaken my old habits either,' said Nagare, flashing a grin over his shoulder.

'You know, this feels like a scene from a movie,' said Koishi, glancing at the two of them. 'Two ageing detectives – partners from back in the day, reunited at last!'

'Hey!' scowled Hideji. 'You could have left out the "ageing" part . . .'

'Koishi, could you come here a moment?' called Nagare from the kitchen.

'Looks like I'm doing the finishing touches,' said Koishi.

'Better do a good job!' teased Hideji as she walked off.

Nagare murmured some instructions to Koishi as she entered the kitchen. Meanwhile, Hideji did as Nagare had told him and began to scan the newspaper's pages, though his attention was really elsewhere. Soon the fragrant aroma of the soup stock wafted through the air. Hideji's nose twitched involuntarily.

'It would have been a slightly different time of day, but I imagine something like this was on the television.' Taking a seat opposite Hideji, Nagare pressed a button on the remote control. Up on the wall, next to the miniature shrine on the shelf, the television began showing the evening news.

'You get home from work. You're too tired to change your clothes, so you just slip off your jacket, loosen your tie and sit yourself down at the low table. You unfold the newspaper, flick on the television, and that's when you notice that special smell coming from the kitchen.' As Nagare painted this scene, Hideji closed his eyes, his face turned up towards the ceiling. 'It was the same for me back then. I'd be so exhausted from work I'd be unable to lift a finger, so hungry I could barely speak. I'd call out to Kikuko, asking when dinner would be ready . . .'

'Oh, it was Chieko who used to scold me,' said Hideji. 'Why put the television on if you're not even going to watch it, she'd say.'

'I imagine you protested that watching it was part of your job.'

'Must have been the same scene in every detective's house.'

After this back-and-forth had continued for a while, Koishi called from the kitchen.

'Dad, I think it might be time to put the egg in!'

'Before you do that, could you sprinkle that stuff in the little ceramic jar into the pot?'

'All of it?'

'All of it. Scatter it all over, then give the soup a good mix with the ladle. Then whack the heat up. Simmer everything for a bit, crack the egg in, then turn the heat off and pop the lid on right away. Not tightly, though – leave it a little askew,' instructed Nagare.

'Timing's everything with nabeyaki-udon, isn't it? When Chieko brought it out, I'd be so absorbed in my newspaper that she'd shout at me.'

'Oh, I can imagine. "Your noodles will turn to mush!" That kind of thing?' said Nagare.

'Here we are!' exclaimed Koishi, bringing over the steaming earthenware pot with a pair of oven gloves.

'What do you reckon? Smells just like back in the day, I'll bet.'

Hideji leaned in and sniffed the pot, then backed off again before the steam got the better of him.

'Oh yes. Nami's version never smells like this,' said Hideji, tilting his head to one side.

'Well, I hope you enjoy!' said Nagare, getting to his feet and heading back into the kitchen with Koishi.

Hideji quickly joined his palms together in a show of gratitude for the meal, then lifted the lid from the earthenware pot. Fragrant steam billowed out. Reaching for the celadon spoon, he began by sipping the broth. He gave a deep nod, then turned his attention to the udon, raising them from the bowl with his chopsticks before slurping them loudly. They were so hot he almost spluttered. Next, he fished some of the negi onion out from the bottom of the pot, arranged it on the noodles, and inserted them into his mouth. He savoured a bite of chicken, then nibbled on the sliced kamaboko. As he did so, Hideji nodded approvingly.

A rush of warmth filled his body, freezing cold just a moment ago, and a light sweat formed on his forehead. He extracted a handkerchief from his jacket pocket and dabbed at his brow and cheeks.

Next, as if only just remembering it was there, he picked up the prawn tempura with his fingers and pinched it in two with his chopsticks, before inserting the head into his mouth.

'Ah, the egg,' muttered Hideji to himself with a smile. He was wondering whether to dip the other half of his tempura into it. 'Choosing when to break the yolk. That's the best part . . .'

Nagare had reappeared at Hideji's side. 'So? How is it?' He sounded somewhat nervous.

'Incredible. Tastes just the way I remember. This is how I asked Nami to make it, but . . .' As he talked, Hideji's chopsticks seemed to keep moving of their own accord.

'Well, things can taste very different depending on how you're feeling,' said Nagare, an understanding look in his eyes. 'I imagine you get all tense when you're eating Nami's food.'

'Yes, you could say that,' said Hideji, dabbing his brow with the handkerchief again.

Nagare sat back down opposite him. 'I mean, I'm sure there are plenty of differences between her version and Chieko's. But if you just relaxed a little more, you'd probably stop noticing them.'

'Okay,' said Hideji, his tone doubtful. 'But this really does taste different. What kind of magic did you use?'

'Not magic, Hideji. Deduction.'

'Is that so?' said Hideji, smiling in between mouthfuls of udon. 'Never could resist a good case, could you?'

'First, I investigated the soup stock – or rather, where Chieko bought the ingredients for it. That was my starting point. I paid a visit to the Junenji temple area and talked to your neighbours. Seems you don't talk to them much, but Chieko certainly did. One woman in particular remembered her very well. Apparently they even used to go shopping together, at the Masugata arcade over in Demachi.'

Nagare spread out a map and pointed to the area in question with a pen.

'Oh, yes. With that famous sweet shop where people line up all day for the mame-mochi,' said Hideji, glancing at the map with his chopsticks still in hand.

'Yes – that's Demachi Futaba. And just next to it is the Masugata shopping arcade. The locals don't shop at touristy places like Nishiki Market – they all go to Masugata. Seems that's where Chieko got most of her ingredients. Kombu and bonito flakes for the soup stock from Fujiya, chicken from Torisen, vegetables from Kaneko . . . She always got her ingredients from the same places. The other housewives in the area still do all their shopping there, too.'

Nagare showed Hideji a pamphlet for the shopping arcade.

'Does it really make that much of a difference where you buy the ingredients?' asked Hideji, relishing a mouthful of chicken.

'Oh yes. The individual differences might be small, but the combined effect in the dish can be pretty noticeable. For example, when she bought ingredients for her stock from Fujiya, she made sure it was top-grade Matsumae kombu, and combined that with Soda bonito flakes and dried mackerel flakes. Then, when she was making up the stock at home, she'd add Urume sardines to the mix. Chieko told your neighbour all about it, apparently.'

'I never realized how much hard work went into that stock. Nami just uses the powdered stuff – no wonder it tastes so different!' said Hideji, picking up a shiitake mushroom with his chopsticks.

'It's not just the dashi stock. See that shiitake you've got there? Chieko would take a batch of them, dry them out in the sun, rehydrate them, and then boil them down with soy and sugar. That way, when you bite into them, you get that wonderful burst of umami.'

'Oh, so it was shiitake she was drying in the garden? Heck of an effort to go to, isn't it! I think Nami just boils them raw,' said Hideji, admiring the flavour of the shiitake.

'Still, Chieko didn't have time to make udon by hand, or fry the tempura herself. You were too impatient for that. Instead she bought fresh noodles and prawn tempura from a little shop named Hanasuzu. Tastes just like it used to, doesn't it? The shop's owner told me they haven't changed their noodle batter or the way they fry the tempura one bit in all these years.'

'Masugata, Hanasuzu, Fujiya . . . Ah, I see! That was what she meant by *masu, suzu, fuji*. She was running through the names of the shops she needed to stop by!'

'She'd put the kombu in the earthenware pot, together with a layer of roughly chopped Kujo negi, then pour in the stock. Once you were sitting down at the table, she'd turn on the stove. When the pot came to the boil she'd add the chicken, and once that was cooked she'd loosen up the udon noodles and add them. Next, she'd add the kamaboko slices, dried wheat cake, shiitake and prawn tempura. Then, right at the end, she'd crack the egg in,' explained Nagare.

'I should write this down,' said Hideji, reaching for his notebook, but Nagare stopped him.

'Don't worry, I'll write it all out for you.'

'I'll have to pass the recipe on to Nami.'

'I should warn you, though. The stock won't taste quite like this.'

'What makes you so sure?' asked Hideji, looking unconvinced. 'I can contact that shop and get them to send the kombu and bonito flakes for the stock. It'll cost a pretty penny, but I don't mind. Nami knows how to cook, so she'll certainly make good use of it.'

'The problem is the water. We get soft water down here, but it's a lot harder up north. That makes it a lot harder to draw the umami out from the kombu. Of course, you could always get water sent up from Kyoto too, but then it'd lose its freshness.'

'Different water, eh . . .' said Hideji, his shoulders drooping slightly.

'Hideji, let's try a little experiment,' said Nagare, getting to his feet and opening the fridge. From inside he took two cups of water and placed them in front of Hideji.

'Try a sip of each.'

'A and B?' said Hideji, looking at the labels on the cups. 'Is this some kind of test?' He tried a sip of each.

'Which tastes better?'

'Well, they're both just water, aren't they? But I think I prefer A. It seems . . . mellower, somehow.' Hideji picked up the cup marked 'A'.

'A is water from a well used by a tofu shop near the Masugata arcade here in Kyoto. B is from the Miyamizu sake brewery, in your hometown of Mikage. So it looks like you've got used to our Kyoto water, Hideji. People always complain about the water when they move somewhere new. But the water's not going to change, is it? You have to adjust your cooking instead. If the water tastes different in Taka-saki, you'll just have to get used to that, too,' said Nagare decisively.

'I see what you mean. Still, I'm glad I got to try this nabeyaki-udon first. I suppose I should savour the taste,' said Hideji, carefully scooping up some of the broth with his spoon.

'You used to eat it almost every day in winter, didn't you?'

'Chieko knew I loved it, and it was something delicious she could always whip up on a cold day.'

'She and Kikuko really stuck with us, didn't they? Even when we were working day and night. Coming home at who knows what hour and demanding food like that – the cheek of it!' Nagare said, looking down at the table.

'Come on, Dad, don't drag the mood down. Hideji is supposed to be starting a whole new life, remember!' said Koishi as she poured them some water. Her eyes appeared slightly moist.

'What's this? Tastes bitter,' said Hideji, retrieving a yellow scrap of something from his mouth.

'That's yuzu peel. I think she added it for the aroma,' explained Nagare.

'Ah, that makes sense.'

'Normally people just sprinkle it on top. But Chieko knew you wouldn't want yuzu peel on top of your udon, so she hid it at the bottom of the pot instead. That way, if you mentioned the bitter taste, she'd know you'd drunk the broth right to the bottom.'

'Nagare, I have to hand it to you. This was some

outstanding detective work. It was exactly the nabeyaki-udon I remembered,' said Hideji, setting down his spoon and pressing his palms together in appreciation.

'Glad to hear it.'

'So, feeling better about moving to Takasaki?' said Koishi.

Hideji nodded in response. 'How much do I owe you for the detective service?' he asked, getting out his wallet.

'Oh, we leave that up to the client. Just transfer us however much you feel it was worth,' said Koishi, passing him a slip of paper with their bank details.

'In that case, I'll make sure to reward you handsomely,' said Hideji, putting on his trench coat.

'I hope we'll see you again soon,' said Nagare, walking him out of the restaurant.

'I'll be coming back to Kyoto a few times a year to visit Chieko's grave. I'll pop by then. Just make sure you have some more delicious grub waiting!'

As Hideji left the restaurant, Drowsy walked over and rubbed up against his feet.

'Be nice to Nami, okay?' said Koishi, scooping up the cat.

'Hideji, you do know what Gunma's famous for, don't you?' Nagare asked.

'Oh yes. Cold, dry winds – and strong-willed women. That's what people say, isn't it?'

'Well, then, sounds like you're ready,' said Nagare with a chuckle.

'Don't go catching a cold now, Hideji!'

'Koishi, you'd better settle down with someone, or your father will never find himself a new wife,' said Hideji.

'Oh, you don't need to tell *me* that,' replied Koishi, pouting.

Just as he was about to set off, Hideji turned around.

'Nagare, there's something I wanted to ask.'

'What's that, then?'

'That bowl of udon. It really did taste just the way it used to. But it seemed a tad . . . saltier, somehow.'

'Must be your imagination. I made the stock exactly the way Chieko did,' replied Nagare with conviction.

'Right, my imagination. Well, thank you, anyway. It was just how I remembered,' said Hideji.

'Take care of yourself, Hideji!' Koishi called to Hideji as he made his way back down Shomen-dori, now enveloped in the blue haze of the gathering dusk.

As Hideji turned around, Nagare bowed deeply and called out to him.

'We'll be wishing you and Nami all the best!'

Back in the restaurant, Koishi began cleaning up.

'I'm so glad he enjoyed that.'

'Moving to an unfamiliar part of the country at that

age – and gaining a new father-in-law to boot. It won't be easy for him,' said Nagare, removing his white apron and draping it over a chair.

'Oh, he'll have fun. The cosy life of a newlywed awaits!'

'I don't know, Koishi. Personally, I'm too old for anything like that. No, it's Kikuko all the way for me.'

'Dad, you forgot to give him that recipe! He's probably still in the neighbourhood – I'll take it to him.'

'Never mind the recipe, Koishi. Hideji can't stay stuck in Kyoto for ever. It's time he moved on from Chieko and learned to enjoy Nami's cooking.'

'But he might come back looking for it!'

'Don't worry. I know what he's like.'

'I sure hope you do . . .'

'Anyway, it's getting on for dinnertime. Aren't you hungry?'

'Let me guess: nabeyaki-udon again?'

'Nope. Tonight we're having udon hotpot!'

'Isn't that basically the same thing?'

'Well, Hiroshi called to say he's got hold of some tasty Akashi sea bream, and that he'd bring it over for us. I thought we could have it as a hotpot.'

'Oh, so we'll eat the sea bream hotpot-style, then add the udon afterwards? Nice. By the way, I wanted to ask – what was it you had me put in Hideji's soup right at the end? You know, that stuff in the jar.'

'Instant dashi powder. He'll need to get used to that stuff if he's going to live with Nami.'

'So that's why he thought the stock was a little saltier than he remembered!'

'Yes. If I can just get him to think that's how Chieko's version always tasted, then even if Nami's version is a little less . . . delicate, he shouldn't notice the difference.'

'But couldn't you have just added it at the start?'

'Well, no – that would have ruined the stock for our hotpot tonight, wouldn't it?'

'Trust you to think of a thing like that, Dad,' said Koishi, slapping Nagare on the back.

'Look – it's snowing.'

'Oh! So it is!'

'Fancy sharing some sake while we watch it fall?'

'Ooh, I know just the right one for that,' said Koishi, extracting a bottle from the fridge.

'Ah, Setchubai. "Plum Blossoms in the Snow". Perfect, and not just because of the name. It's a little sweet, but it'll go very well with the hotpot. Kikuko would have loved it,' said Nagare, looking fondly in the direction of the altar.

36

Chapter 2:
Beef Stew

1

The ginkgo trees in front of Higashi Honganji temple had lost all their leaves.

It was December, and the two elderly women in brightly coloured kimonos making their way past the monks bustling around the temple made for an eye-catching sight. An employee who had just emerged from a religious clothing shop on Shomen-dori, clutching a large cardboard box, stared at them as if thinking: who on earth are *they*?

Striding along at a pace wholly out of keeping with their traditional attire, they eventually came to a halt in front of a nondescript, shabby-looking building.

'So this is the place with the detective who'll help me find that dish?'

Nobuko Nadaya, a wisteria-coloured cape around her shoulders, was staring open-mouthed at the building.

'Yes. There's no sign, but it's called the Kamogawa Diner,' replied Tae Kurusu, pulling the sliding aluminium door open. Nobuko reluctantly followed her into the restaurant.

'Come on in! We were worried about you, Tae – it's getting late!' said Koishi Kamogawa, flashing a smile. She was wearing a white apron on top of a black trouser suit.

'We stopped to pray at Higashi on the way. Couldn't just walk past it, could we?' said Tae, removing her auburn shawl and draping it over the back of a chair.

From the kitchen peered Nagare Kamogawa. 'You must be cold!'

'Ah, Nagare, let me introduce you. This is Nobuko Nadaya, an old school friend of mine.' Prompted by a nudge in the back from Tae, Nobuko bowed her head demurely.

'Nagare Kamogawa. This is my daughter, Koishi.' Nagare had emerged from the kitchen, and wiped his hands on his apron as he bowed.

'I'm impressed you found us,' said Koishi, glancing at Nobuko and Tae in turn.

'Well, now that you mention it, you need to do something about that half-baked advert of yours!' snapped Tae. 'I managed to work it out because Nobuko here showed me a copy of *Gourmet Monthly* and I happened to recognize the name Kamogawa. Without that, there's no way any normal person could find their way here with only the advert to guide them.'

'And yet here you are. Must be fate, don't you think? You know, I rather like the idea of connecting with people through a one-line advertisement in a magazine,' said Nagare, pursing his lips.

'Well, we're here now. That's the important thing!' Nobuko interceded.

'Thank you, Nobuko,' said Nagare. 'You seem the quiet type – at least compared to Tae here!'

'My, how rude!' exclaimed Tae, her nostrils twitching.

'The two of us might seem like chalk and cheese, but we've always been very close,' said Nobuko glancing sideways at Tae.

'So, what can I get you to drink?' asked Koishi.

'It's a bit chilly, isn't it – fancy a bottle of hot sake?' said Tae to Nobuko.

'Oh, let's not drink this afternoon,' replied Nobuko, as if admonishing her.

'What's the matter, Nobuko? Feeling out of sorts?'

'No, nothing like that. I'm just not quite in the mood today.' Nobuko looked down at the table.

'Well, it's not quite the dim sum you requested, but I think this should be just the thing to fill you up,' said Nagare, placing a bento box in front of Tae.

'Sorry for being so demanding,' she said, and bowed slightly.

'Dad got quite nervous when he heard you were bringing a friend,' said Koishi in her ear. 'He was worried he might embarrass you!'

'You didn't have to tell her that!' said Nagare, glowering at Koishi as he placed another bento box in front of Nobuko.

'But this is . . .' Nobuko's eyes widened at the sight of the black lacquered box.

'Traditional Wajima ware,' said Nagare.

'You see, Nobuko, even the bento boxes are special. Are you beginning to see why I spoke so highly of this place?' said Tae, proudly puffing out her chest.

Nobuko's eyes lit up as she removed the lid. 'It's not just the box, either . . . Look inside!'

'How beautiful,' said Tae, her gaze darting from one part of the bento to the next.

'I'll guide you through it,' said Nagare. 'See how it's partitioned into four? In the top right is a selection of smaller appetizers. In the bottom right is the grilled fish of the day – in this case, teriyaki yellowtail. Top left is a selection of sashimi and pickled dishes: Akashi sea bream, Kishu tuna, and flash-grilled Karatsu abalone. Seared Miyajima conger eel, served with pickled cucumber and myoga ginger. And in the bottom left is the matsutake rice – the mushrooms are from Shinshu, and wonderfully fragrant. I'll bring some soup over shortly. In the meantime, enjoy!'

Nagare bowed and turned back to the kitchen.

'Let's tuck in,' said Tae, joining her hands together in appreciation before reaching for her chopsticks.

'It's delicious,' said Nobuko, who had already reached into the bento and sampled the sea bream.

'The sashimi looks wonderful, but these appetizers are simply exquisite. Let's see . . . rolled barracuda sushi, dashi-maki omelette, and those look like quail tsukune balls. And this simmered octopus – it just melts on your tongue!' Tae's mouth was agape with delight.

'I don't think I've had a bento this nice since those Tsujitomi ones we had at the tea ceremony. How many years ago was that?' asked Nobuko, extending her chopsticks in the direction of the octopus.

'You're right. Those were certainly something, but these are just as good. Ah, the aromas!' Tae closed her eyes as she savoured a mouthful of the matsutake rice.

'No need to overdo the compliments – they'll go to his head!' said Koishi, pouring tea into their cups and glancing towards the kitchen.

'Oh, Nobuko – this young lady is the head of the detective agency. Koishi, she'll fill you in shortly if that's okay?' said Tae, putting down her chopsticks and becoming rather serious.

'All I really do is conduct the initial interview. It's my dad who does the real detective work,' said Koishi bashfully.

'Here's your soup!' said Nagare, setting a bowl down next to each of the bento boxes.

'And what have we here?' asked Tae, removing the lid from the Negoro lacquerware bowl.

'Tilefish and crab meat broth. It's chilly these days, so I grated some kudzu in to thicken it up – you know, make it a little more warming. Please, enjoy while it's hot,' replied Nagare, tucking his tray under his arm.

'The yuzu has a wonderful aroma, too,' said Nobuko, bringing the bowl close to her nose.

'That's from a village called Mizuo in the mountains west of Kyoto. Fragrant, isn't it? Well, I'll leave you to it.'

'This grated kudzu really adds something,' said Tae to Koishi, cupping the bowl in her hands. 'Piping hot – and delicious.'

'Nice subtle flavour, isn't it?' replied Koishi, practically drooling as she watched. 'We make a hotpot version of it sometimes. Put lightly seared tilefish and crab in the bottom of the pot, then add some dashi stock and plenty of grated turnip. Season it with some shichimi spice and yuzu, and it'll warm you right through.'

'I suppose we should eat up!' said Tae to Nobuko, as if to bring the conversation to a close.

'There's also dessert – sorry, I mean the mizugashi

course. So please take your time,' said Koishi, shrugging her shoulders.

'That's right, Koishi. There's no such thing as "dessert" in Japanese cuisine. The fruit served at the end of the meal is called mizugashi. We're not in France, after all!' said Tae, her nostrils flaring.

'Really, Tae, you never change, do you? Always fussing over the strangest things . . . I'm not sure it really matters,' said Nobuko, setting down her bowl.

'No, it *does* matter. If you mess around with language like that, it's culture that suffers. Traditional Japanese sweet dishes are in decline precisely because people insist on calling them English words like "dessert"!'

Nobuko watched Tae put a piece of yellowtail in her mouth, skin and all, and decided to follow suit. 'I wonder how many years it's been since the two of us had a nice meal like this together,' she said, changing the subject.

'Why, we had that eel at Nodaiwa in Yokohama just three months ago. We drank plenty that day, too!' replied Tae, setting down her chopsticks and taking a sip of tea.

'Oh yes. I'd forgotten all about that. I've been living in a bit of a daze for the past few months, you see.'

'Because of this dish you're after?'

'Yes. It was around six months ago that it all came back to me.' Nobuko finished eating and replaced the lid on her bento box.

'Can I bring you some matcha tea?' Koishi asked Tae in a curious tone of voice, as she brought over the fruit.

'Not today, thank you. I think Nobuko here is in a hurry.'

Nobuko nodded slightly as if to confirm what her friend had said.

'Oh – is that a Daishiro persimmon?' asked Tae. 'I thought they were finished for the year.'

'Dai-shir-o?' repeated Nobuko, spoon in hand.

'I suppose you don't get them much up in Tokyo,' said Tae, inserting her spoon into the fruit.

'And this Baccarat plate! The persimmon is so vivid against the crystal.'

'Not just any Baccarat either. This looks like their Harumi collection. You don't see it very often – even at high-end kaiseki restaurants. Koishi, how on earth did it find its way *here*?'

Koishi smiled at Tae's question. 'It's Dad's pride and joy. He has plenty more like it, too. Mum always scolded him for buying them. *How much was the loan on that one, then*, she used to say!'

'Koishi, quit talking nonsense and go get ready,' said Nagare, emerging from the kitchen.

'Yes, *father*, I'm on it!' said Koishi, pointedly shrugging her shoulders before removing her white apron. 'Nobuko, I'll be waiting for you in the back office.'

'That daughter of mine really is impossible sometimes.

The mouth on her!' said Nagare, watching Koishi make her exit.

'Such a lovely girl. Always saying such *clever* things!' said Tae. There was the slightest hint of sarcasm in her tone.

'Enjoy the food?' Nagare asked Nobuko as he cleared away the bento boxes.

'Oh, it was delicious. I've always wanted to eat here, given how much Tae seems to like it,' said Nobuko, eliciting a chuckle from her friend.

'Well, Nobuko, shall I show you to the office? And Tae, do you mind waiting here?' asked Nagare, looking at the clock on the wall. Nobuko glanced sideways at Tae, then got reluctantly to her feet. She walked a few steps behind Nagare as he led the way. After a moment, he stopped and turned. 'Having second thoughts, are we?'

'Just feeling a little . . . nervous,' said Nobuko, looking down at the floor. 'Now that I'm here and everything.'

'Well, you've come all this way. Might as well at least have a little chat!'

Nagare turned away and set off again. Nobuko walked slowly behind him, looking at the photographs that filled the walls.

'This is mainly food I've cooked. Though there are a few other old photos mixed in there,' explained Nagare. Nobuko remained silent, her eyes glued to one photo in particular.

'Oh, that's a crossing on the Eizan line,' said Nagare, following Nobuko's gaze. 'My wife and I took the photo to commemorate our first ride on it together. Well, here we are!' Nagare opened the door to reveal two sofas facing each other. Koishi was already seated on the one furthest away.

'Come on in!' she called.

Nobuko slowly walked into the room.

'Oh, there's no need to sit right at the end like that! Pop yourself in the middle. I don't bite, I promise!' said Koishi with a grin.

'Sorry – I'm just not used to this.'

'Oh, I don't think anyone is! Now, if you could just write your name, age, date of birth, address and contact details down here . . .'

Koishi placed a folder on the low table between them. With what seemed like sudden resolve, Nobuko began scribbling away.

'What beautiful handwriting you have!'

'You say the most charming things,' said Nobuko, returning the folder.

'So, what kind of dish are you looking for?' said Koishi, opening her notebook as she cut to the chase.

'Actually, I don't really remember. You see, it's something I've only eaten once – and it was over fifty years ago,' replied Nobuko, a perplexed look on her face.

'Well, tell me what you *do* remember. Was it meat, fish or vegetables?'

'I think it was some kind of stewed meat and vegetables.'

'Japanese-style or Western-style?'

'Western. Now that I think about it, it might have been a beef stew.'

'And where did you eat it? In a restaurant?'

After a short pause, Nobuko replied: 'Yes, a restaurant. In Kyoto.'

'Which restaurant in Kyoto?'

'*That* I don't remember at all.'

'How about even a rough location?'

'I'm sorry, I just can't seem to . . .' Nobuko looked down at the low table.

'Even the slightest hint will go a long way.'

'The thing is, I had such a big shock while I was eating it that I've lost all memory of what happened before and after. And before I knew it, I was back at my uncle's house . . .'

'And where was that?'

'Kitahama.'

'That's not in Kyoto, is it?' Koishi looked up from her notebook.

'No, Osaka.'

'Okay, but it was at a restaurant in Kyoto that you ate this beef stew . . . Would you mind telling me a little more about that shock you mentioned?' said Koishi, glancing encouragingly at Nobuko.

'In 1957, about fifty-five years ago, I was attending a women's college in Yokohama. That's where I became friends with Tae. I was studying Japanese classical literature. You know – *The Tale of Genji, The Ten Foot Square Hut, The Tale of the Heike* . . . I just found it all so fascinating. Around that time, I read a paper by a student researching the same field at Kyoto University, and we seemed to have similar interests, so I decided to write to him. We exchanged a few letters after that, and then it was here in Kyoto that we met for the first time. I happened to be staying with my uncle in Osaka for a week, you see.' Nobuko drank all her tea in one gulp, as if to quench her thirst.

'So that was your first meeting – and your first date,' said Koishi, her eyes widening.

'I suppose nowadays people would call it a date, wouldn't they? I just thought of it as a chance to exchange our opinions about literature!'

'But the two of you hit it off?'

'Yes, I suppose we did. We got completely wrapped up in a conversation about *The Ten Foot Square Hut*. Actually, it was mainly him telling me all sorts of interesting things about it.' A dreamlike look came over Nobuko as Koishi scribbled away.

'It wasn't just the conversation you found interesting, was it? Sounds like you were quite taken with the young man, too,' said Koishi without looking up from her notebook. Nobuko's cheeks turned red with an almost girlish embarrassment.

'Well, I don't know about that . . .'

'I'm still wondering what it was that you found so shocking,' said Koishi with a puzzled expression.

'Well, you have to remember that in those days, people couldn't act as freely as they can now. So when, after our long conversation, he asked me if I'd join him for dinner, I have to admit I was quite unsure. It all seemed a little improper.'

'Gosh. I'm sure glad *I* wasn't born that long ago,' blurted Koishi, before hurriedly covering her mouth as if trying to take her words back.

'Anyway, I was already feeling rather overwhelmed by it all. Then, while we were eating, he suddenly asked me a rather different question, and I completely panicked.'

'What, did he ask you out?' asked Koishi, peering at Nobuko.

'Oh, I don't think I'd have dashed out of the restaurant over something like that.'

'Wait . . . He didn't *propose*, did he?' asked Koishi, her eyes widening. Rather than denying or confirming this suggestion, Nobuko simply turned her head and remained silent.

Koishi leaned forward. 'Well, what did you say?'

'I didn't even answer. I just ran right out of there,' replied Nobuko, her eyes downcast.

'And what became of the young man?'

'I don't know. I never saw him again.'

'Wow. So, he proposed to you, and to this day, fifty-five years later, you haven't heard a thing from him?' Koishi leaned back on the sofa.

'Well, what would you have done?' asked Nobuko, finally looking up.

'I'm sorry. You didn't come here for a therapy session, did you. It's that beef stew you wanted us to find. Could you tell me a little more about it?' asked Koishi, sitting up again.

'I'd only managed half of it before I ran out of the restaurant, so I really don't remember it very well.'

'Hmm. I wonder how many places were serving beef stew in Kyoto in 1957 . . .' said Koishi, half to herself, as she jotted down another note.

'Potatoes and carrots,' murmured Nobuko, her voice barely audible.

'Sorry, what was that?' Koishi's ears had pricked up, pen ready in her hand.

'When he'd taken our order, the chef started peeling potatoes and carrots, and then he put them in a big pot . . .' replied Nobuko, her eyes closed.

'Must have taken a while! I wonder if the customers minded waiting like that. Couldn't he have just warmed up some stew he'd made earlier?' asked Koishi, a doubtful expression on her face.

'While we were waiting for our food, this wonderful smell came wafting over,' said Nobuko, her gaze drifting across the ceiling as she recalled the scene.

'And you're sure he wasn't just asking you out?'

'At first I thought he might be. When the food finally arrived, and I tried a mouthful, I couldn't believe how good it tasted. I remember thinking I'd never had anything like it. My father did like his meat, and we'd had stews at home before, but this was on a whole different level. The flavour was wonderfully rich, without being too overwhelming. Then, about halfway through our meal, he suddenly came out with . . .'

'The proposal. Then you got up and dashed out of there. By the way, what was his name?'

'Nemoto,' said Nobuko, looking up at the ceiling again. 'Or Nejima. No, wait, maybe it was Nekawa . . .'

Koishi was dumbfounded. 'You've forgotten the name of the man who proposed to you?'

Nobuko nodded. 'The only part I'm sure about is the *ne*, because it means "mouse" and he kept joking about how he was born in the year of the mouse. Oh, and I'm pretty certain he lived in Kamigyo Ward.'

Koishi scribbled away.

'I must have looked rather out of sorts when I got back to my uncle's house in Osaka, because he and my aunt asked me what had happened. I ended up confessing everything.

They immediately got in touch with my parents, who made me get rid of all his letters and everything else to do with him. I remember thinking I just needed to erase him from my memory.'

'Well, it sounds like tracking him down will be our best bet,' said Koishi, giving her pen a good shake. 'I could do with another hint. Anything will help. Where did you go before the restaurant, for example?'

'Before the restaurant . . . I think we walked a lot . . . Ah, yes, we were walking in a forest. A deep, dark forest.'

'A forest,' said Koishi, recording this detail in her notebook. 'Well, Kyoto is surrounded by mountains on three sides, and they're all covered in trees, so I'm afraid that doesn't help me much . . .'

'Oh – when we came out of the forest there was a shrine. We prayed there, and then . . .'

'Kyoto has a pretty endless amount of shrines next to forests, too,' said Koishi, still scribbling away. 'I do appreciate you trying to remember everything. But with this little to go on, even Dad might struggle . . .' She sighed as she leafed through the pages of her notebook.

'It's going to be tricky, then?' asked Nobuko, her shoulders drooping.

'Can I ask what made you want to eat this beef stew again after all these years?'

Nobuko sighed again. 'I have a daughter, you see. She

52

turned forty this year, but she's still single. I think she's always been reluctant to leave me on my own, what with my husband dying early and everything. Anyway, about six months ago, someone proposed to her.'

A twinkle came into her eyes as she continued. 'She told me she wasn't sure whether to accept. Then she asked me how my husband had proposed. I didn't know what to tell her. Ours was an arranged marriage, so there was never the opportunity for that kind of thing. No – all that came to *my* mind when I heard the word "proposal" was . . .'

'That day fifty-five years ago.'

Nobuko nodded. 'When I didn't even manage to reply. Of course, it's not like I can give him an answer after all these years, but I do find myself wondering what my life would have been like if I'd stayed in that restaurant and finished my meal.'

'This has all been very helpful. Let's hope Dad can find that beef stew!' said Koishi, snapping her notebook shut.

'Thank you very much,' said Nobuko, bowing her head and then hesitantly getting to her feet.

When they returned down the corridor to the restaurant, they found Nagare and Tae sitting opposite each other, deep in conversation.

'Well?' asked Tae. 'Did you tell Koishi all about the stew?'

'Yes. She was very nice and thorough,' replied Nobuko, her expression still somewhat dazed.

'Have you scheduled Nobuko's next visit, then, Koishi?' asked Nagare.

'Oops, I forgot the most important part. Nobuko – it normally takes us about two weeks to track down the dish in question and serve it up to you. How does coming back in a fortnight sound?'

'Yes, that'll be fine,' replied Nobuko readily.

'I'll send a reminder closer to the time,' said Koishi, putting her folder and notebook down on the table.

'So, how much do I owe you?' asked Nobuko, opening her handbag.

'For the detective service, we take payment on delivery, so that can wait until your next visit. As for your meal . . .' Koishi glanced at her father.

'Tae here has already paid for the two of you,' said Nagare.

'Oh no, that won't do! We'll pay separately!' said Nobuko, holding her purse out.

'You paid last time, remember? That expensive eel we had!' said Tae, getting to her feet as if to signal the end of the exchange.

'I'm glad we could have such a leisurely chat,' said Nagare, looking at Tae.

'Oh, me too. Though I'm afraid I may have said too much,' said Tae, glancing sideways at Nobuko.

'Not again! Drowsy, you can't just come wandering in here!' The tabby cat had strolled through the door as soon as Koishi opened it.

'Listen here, you,' said Nagare, glaring at the cat. 'These two are wearing beautiful kimonos, so don't even think about going near them.'

Tae and Nobuko left the restaurant and began slowly strolling west. Nagare and Koishi watched their figures recede until they turned a corner.

'I think this one might be a little tricky, Dad,' said Koishi, holding out her notebook.

'Well, it's never exactly easy,' replied Nagare from across the restaurant table where they were sitting, as he opened the notebook.

'It's a beef stew she wants us to recreate, but it's a little complicated. Nobuko's memory is . . . patchy,' said Koishi, glancing at the page Nagare was studying and pointing to her notes.

'Beef stew, eh?' said Nagare. 'I haven't eaten that in a while. And what's this . . . *A shrine next to a forest*, okay. *Only started peeling the vegetables once they'd ordered. Born*

in the year of the mouse. Uncle's house in Kitahama, Osaka.
Koishi, what on earth . . .'

'Reckon you can do it?'

'You're going to have to give me a few more details,' said
Nagare, propping his head in his hands.

Koishi relayed everything Nobuko had told her. Nagare
nodded along, taking notes of his own. When he remained
silent, Koishi peered at him.

'The beef stew itself shouldn't be too hard to recreate,'
said Nagare, his gaze still tilted down at the notebook.

'Really?' asked Koishi, her eyes widening.

'That's not the hard part,' replied Nagare with a frown.

'But there's a hitch?' Koishi's expression was quizzical.

'Oh, just a few things to figure out,' said Nagare vaguely,
getting to his feet. 'First of all, let's track down that stew.'

2

With the final days of December looming, a strange pres-
sure seemed to fill the air as the inhabitants of Kyoto made
their preparations for the New Year. Everyone passing by
the Kamogawa Diner seemed preoccupied, their pace hastier
than usual.

'I did tell Tae to be here at twelve sharp, you know,' said
Nobuko, sitting at a table near the entrance and occasionally
glancing anxiously out of the window.

Koishi laid a place mat in front of her, together with a set of cutlery.

'She rang just now. Says she had a visitor just as she was about to leave,' said Nagare, poking his head in from the kitchen.

'She could have just told them she had important business,' grumbled Nobuko.

'Nobuko, about today's dish . . .' began Nagare, emerging from the kitchen and standing in front of her. She looked up apprehensively and waited for him to go on.

'I managed to track down the dish in question. But I want everything to be just as it was fifty-five years ago. So, please imagine you just walked into that restaurant and placed your order.'

'Alright, I will.' With an obedient nod, Nobuko slowly closed her eyes, as if mentally turning back the hands of a clock.

'I'll be making the dish today. Dad made sure I got the recipe just right,' said Koishi, making her way towards the kitchen. Nagare, meanwhile, seated himself in front of Nobuko.

'You ate your stew at a restaurant named Furuta Grill. It's down a narrow alley, nestled under the leaves of a black locust tree. There's a counter on your right as you walk in. You and the gentleman in question would have sat there, side by side. He tells the chef your order. *Two bowls of beef stew, please.* The chef starts peeling potatoes and carrots, working away at a leisurely pace. And you're sitting here, waiting.' Nagare spoke slowly, in a low voice, almost as if he was trying to hypnotize her.

'But . . . how did you . . .'

'Well, it wasn't just the beef stew I went looking for. I ended up retracing that whole day you spent in Kyoto.'

'The whole day . . .' said Nobuko, gazing up at the ceiling.

'Winter, fifty-five years ago. I imagine it was a chilly day just like today. I believe you and this gentleman would have arranged to meet at Sanjo station on the Keihan line. He probably wanted to show you Shimogamo Shrine. These days, the train runs all the way to Demachiyanagi, but back then you had to walk north along the banks of the Kamogawa.'

Nagare unfolded a map of Kyoto. Nobuko leaned forward and watched as he traced their route.

'Ah, that's right. We followed the river upstream. The conversation flowed so easily it seemed hard to believe we'd never met in person before . . .' Nobuko was beginning to blush.

'This is Demachiyanagi. You probably made your way up onto the embankment here, then headed into the Tadasu Forest,' said Nagare, running his finger across the green expanse that unfolded above the Y-shaped confluence of the

Takanogawa and Kamogawa rivers. 'That must be the forest you remembered walking through.'

'But I don't remember it being so close to the city. I recall it being a wilder sort of forest than that . . .' said Nobuko, cocking her head slightly.

'Oh, the Tadasu Forest is pretty wild. It's virginal woodland – practically untouched,' said Nagare, opening up a laptop and turning the screen towards Nobuko. On it she could see the vermilion torii gate of a shrine.

'This is Shimogamo Shrine – the one you must have visited after your walk. It's the only one you'd reach in the way you described – after walking through a dense forest.'

'But surely there must be other shrines you could arrive at through that forest?' said Nobuko, her tone sceptical.

'The two of you had been discussing *The Ten Foot Square Hut*, hadn't you? In which case, it would make sense for you to visit the shrine associated with that work – the Shimogamo Shrine. There's another reason, too. This gentleman you were with – you said you remembered him being born in the year of the mouse, didn't you? Why would you remember that?'

'Oh, I can't say I know. I imagine it was just something he told me . . .' said Nobuko, a searching look in her eyes.

'You can't even remember the gentleman's name, but you remember his zodiac animal. Now, I reckon that's because it's not his words you're remembering, but an image: that of him praying to the mouse god.'

'The mouse god?'

'Shimogamo Shrine is unusual, even for Kyoto, in that you pray in different places depending on your zodiac animal. There are seven little shrines, known as kotosha. Five of them are dedicated to two animals, and the other two just one. The mouse and the horse each get their own shrine. That'll be why you remember that he was born in the year of the mouse.'

'Ah, yes,' said Nobuko. 'I remember walking up the gravel path and under the red torii gates, expecting to find a big building where we'd pray, and instead there were all these little shrines . . .'

'Images like that never fade, do they?'

'After we left the shrine, we carried on walking along side by side.'

It seemed Nobuko's memories were beginning to return. Nagare watched her closely.

'Koishi,' Nagare called into the kitchen. 'Once you've put the roux in, bring the whole pot through here, would you?'

'When it's almost ready, you mean?' said Koishi, bringing through the aluminium pot with a handle, billowing with fragrant steam.

'Furuta Grill had an open kitchen, so when you were sitting at the counter, you'd have been able to smell something like this,' explained Nagare, holding the pot out towards Nobuko.

'Ah . . . Yes! That's it. That's how it smelled!' said Nobuko, her nose twitching.

'It'll be ready in fifteen minutes or so.'

After glancing at Nobuko, who had closed her eyes, Nagare signalled to Koishi that she should take the pot back to the kitchen.

'Now,' he continued, 'this is going to get a little personal, so please feel free to stop me at any time.'

Nobuko seemed to think for a moment, then nodded slowly.

'Last time you were here, and I showed you to the office, do you remember how you hesitated slightly? When a client does that, it usually means the dish they're looking for is associated with someone they'd rather not remember.'

Nagare stopped to take a sip of his tea. Nobuko's gaze was still fixed on the table.

'Tracking down the recipe for this beef stew in itself wasn't too hard. It's a well-known restaurant, and various critics have written about the place. The route you were walking led right to it. There's just one thing that's been bothering me. Is it really right for me to track someone down and tell you all about them, when it seems you'd rather forget?'

At this, Nobuko looked up and gave a nod of approval.

'His name was Shigeru Nejima. I asked one of the regular customers at Furuta Grill if they remembered a Kyoto University student with the character for "mouse" in his name. Turned out they did.'

'Shigeru Nejima . . .' said Nobuko, a stunned look on her face.

For a moment, Nagare looked her in the eye. Then, as if regaining her senses, Nobuko sat up in her chair.

'Mr Nejima was studying literature at the university. Born and raised in Kyoto. Back then, he lived in the Shinnyodomae neighbourhood of Kamigyo Ward. You know, not far from the Imperial Palace,' said Nagare, pointing at a map in his notebook.

'But . . . how did you find all this out?'

'Actually, it was his daughter who filled me in.'

'He has a daughter?' said Nobuko, her shoulders sagging slightly.

'Let's go back fifty-five years, shall we?' said Nagare, quenching his thirst with another sip of tea before he went on. 'You and Mr Nejima met in December of 1957. In the early days of the New Year, he left Japan for England.'

'England?'

'He was an exchange student there, then ended up staying on at the university. He was there thirty-five years in the end, eventually rising to the rank of honorary professor. He married three years after arriving and had a single daughter. His wife died of an illness five years ago, but even after that he kept up his study of Japanese literature – until his own death, a year ago. I suppose he wanted to take you to London with him. You were living in Yokohama at the time, so he didn't know if he'd get another chance to ask you.'

'But . . . Nagare, this is all just speculation, isn't it?'

'Not exactly. See, his daughter was kind enough to let me read Mr Nejima's diaries. It was all there. He'd kept a diary from 1955 onwards. I imagine he wasn't too keen on his wife reading it, because he always kept it at his university office. His daughter found it after he passed away, when she was sorting through his research materials.'

Nagare smiled gently at Nobuko. 'Of course, he didn't go as far as recording the recipe for the beef stew.' He glanced at the clock on the wall, then turned back towards the kitchen.

'I think I was just . . . afraid,' said Nobuko, choosing her words slowly, as though addressing Nejima himself. 'The idea of happiness pitching up in my life like that all of a sudden – it terrified me.'

'Sorry I'm late!' said Tae, panting as she burst into the restaurant.

'Ah, you're just in time for the stew!' called Koishi from the kitchen.

'Someone popped by unannounced,' explained Tae,

steadying her breathing as she adjusted the neck of her kimono.

Nagare brought the beef stew over and placed it in front of them.

'Oh, that does smell lovely,' said Tae, leaning forward. Nobuko, meanwhile, remained motionless and simply stared at the dish.

'Please, enjoy it while it's hot.'

They did as Nagare suggested, each pressing their palms together in appreciation before reaching for their knife and fork.

Koishi came out from the kitchen and stood alongside Nagare. They watched keenly as the two women tucked in to the food.

Nobuko began by trying a piece of beef, which she chewed slowly for a moment before nodding deeply.

'Oh yes. This is exactly how it tasted.'

'Phew!' said Koishi, then clapped her father on the shoulder. 'Good job, Dad!'

'The broth is very delicate,' said Tae, beaming. 'But it has a wonderfully rich flavour. I imagine you took a great deal of care with the demi-glace sauce.'

'A famous food writer once said the beef stew at Furuta Grill tastes almost like pot-au-feu, but I actually think it's a little different. I imagine they were referring to that delicateness you just mentioned, which comes from using a light tomato-based demi-glace rather than the usual thicker kind. The meat is pre-cooked in stock and quickly simmered with port wine. Put it in a pot with the vegetables, add the demi-glace and cook everything down, and this is the result. If you just chuck the vegetables in with the beef from the start, they lose their shape and all the flavours get confused. But do it Furuta-style and the sauce will simply coat the meat. That way, the umami from the beef and the flavour of the demi-glace only come together once they're in your mouth.' There was a note of pride in Nagare's voice.

'Dad, I tried some, and – wow!' whispered Koishi in his ear.

'What did you expect? I went all out with this one!' he murmured back.

Nobuko and Tae chatted away, leisurely enjoying their meal. When they'd finished, Nagare joined them again.

'Now, I believe this stew will have tasted differently to each of you.'

'What do you mean?' said Tae, dabbing at her mouth with a napkin.

'Well, unlike you, Nobuko sat here for half an hour waiting for her meal. All that time spent in anticipation can only have added to the flavour. I think the "spice" of nostalgia has been at work today.' Nagare gazed kindly at Nobuko.

'Where was Mr Nejima laid to rest?' asked Nobuko, a slight blush coming to her cheeks.

'Konkai Komyoji temple. He died in December of last year. It was a cold day, I'm told.'

Hearing this, Nobuko pursed her lips. 'I acted so rudely back then. And now I'll never be able to apologize . . .'

'Oh, it was just a misunderstanding,' sighed Koishi.

'I suppose we should be on our way,' said Nobuko, extracting her purse from her handbag, perhaps as a way of steadying her emotions.

'We let our clients choose the fee. Just transfer whatever feels right to this account,' said Koishi, handing her a slip of paper.

'That was a wonderful beef stew,' said Tae, bowing to Nagare, who grinned back.

'I'm glad it was to your liking. Though I imagine there was a little more "spice" at work in Nobuko's dish . . .'

'Thank you very much,' said Nobuko as she and Tae left the restaurant.

'Oh, I almost forgot,' said Nagare, reaching into the pocket of his white chef's jacket. 'I have a little something for you.' He pulled out a white envelope the size of a small book. 'Mr Nejima's daughter sent me these.'

Nagare extracted two handkerchiefs from the envelope and showed them to Nobuko.

'Oh, my . . .' gasped Nobuko.

'It seems you left one of these in that restaurant fifty-five years ago. The other one is a present Mr Nejima had been planning to give you. It's Swatow lace, I believe – beautiful, isn't it? The design is titled "The Disc of the Moon" – apparently it was inspired by the poem "Midnight Song" by the Tang-era poet Li Bai. I looked it up, and it turns out it's about longing for someone who's a great distance away. Mr Nejima tried sending it to your family home, together with the one you left in the restaurant, but they refused to accept it. You must have been out at the time. And so he never managed to reconnect with you . . .'

Nagare returned the handkerchiefs to the envelope and handed it to Nobuko.

'Thank you.' She gripped the envelope tightly. As she stared in surprise at the sender's name, a single tear made its way down her cheek.

'Oh, my. What a tasteful gift,' said Tae, dabbing at her eyes with her own handkerchief.

Tae and Nobuko slowly made their way off down the street. Koishi and Nagare stood in front of the restaurant and watched them disappear from view.

Back in the restaurant, they finished cleaning up, then set about preparing dinner.

'I saw the envelope, Dad. I can't believe he named his daughter Nobuko!' said Koishi as they made their way into the living room. 'I hope *you* didn't have some lover in the past who you named me after . . .'

'Oh, come on. It's your mother all the way for me. Right, Kikuko?' Nagare turned and smiled at the portrait on the altar.

'Mum, don't let this guy fool you. You never know with men!'

'See, Koishi, this is why you still can't find a husband.'

'Not *can't*, Dad – *don't want to*. Have you seen the men out there? They're all useless!'

'Oh, shush. Time to get supper ready. Can't keep your mother waiting. Beef stew and wine was always one of her favourite meals. Wasn't it, Kikuko?'

'Dad, wait – what? That wine looks super expensive!'

'Well observed.'

'How did you even afford it?'

'A certain client paid us very handsomely for our services.'

'Well, I can't wait to taste it. What's it called? Not that I'll recognize the name . . .'

'It's a Château Mouton Rothschild. From the year your mother was born – 1958. Apparently Dalí did the drawing on the label. Expensive, but cheaper than the '59. Nothing too lavish. It cost about the same as that laptop I got you.'

'What? You mean a single bottle cost a hundred thousand yen?'

'So what if it did? Your mother never properly splashed out on things, you know.'

'You know, Dad, you can be a bit drastic sometimes.'

'Well, today's the anniversary of your mother's death. Don't tell me you forgot?'

'Of course not. Here you go, Mum,' said Koishi, untying a bouquet of flowers. 'Christmas roses. Her favourite.' She placed them on the small table in front of the altar.

'Getting a bit chilly, isn't it?' said Nagare, looking out of the window.

'Would have been nice if the first snow had fallen today. Mum loved the snow, didn't she?' Koishi turned towards the altar and closed her eyes, pressing her palms tightly together.

Chapter 3:
Mackerel Sushi

1

Sitting in the back of the taxi he'd hailed from Kyoto station, Tomomi Iwakura rubbed his stomach repeatedly. The bento he'd eaten while taking a business call on the bullet train was still firmly lodged in his stomach. And yet, here he was, on his way to a restaurant. He slightly regretted not bringing his usual indigestion medicine.

Tomomi got out of the taxi on Karasuma-dori, cast his gaze about for a moment, and then carefully removed his black-rimmed glasses and looked up at the ginkgo tree that stood in front of Higashi Honganji temple.

Its leaves were all a golden hue. Only now did Tomomi realize just how autumnal the scenery was becoming. There was nowhere like Kyoto to make you really notice the changing of the seasons – something that completely escaped him when he was busy with his work in Tokyo.

The light turned green. He put his glasses back on and made his way across the pedestrian crossing, gazing at his feet as he walked. Then he glanced left and then right along Shomen-dori, his eyes restlessly taking in the sights. The narrow street was lined with shops selling Buddhist altar fittings and religious clothing, and a mix of other businesses and apartments. Just as the taxi driver had insisted, there was no sign of the restaurant he was looking for.

A black luxury sedan, which had been closely following the taxi, passed by and then stopped at the side of the road, as though waiting for him to make his move. With a dismissive glance in its direction, Tomomi quietly tutted and set off again at a brisk pace.

An old woman was making her way down the street towards him, hunched over a pushcart.

'Don't suppose you know of any restaurants around here?' he asked as she passed.

'A restaurant?' replied the old woman, straightening up to look at him. 'There's one on the next street down. The Daiya, it's called. Is that the place you're after?'

'Ah, no, that's not quite right.'

At this, the old woman pointed to a delivery truck. 'Try asking that young man instead. I'm clueless about this sort of thing!'

Tomomi trotted across the street to where the truck was parked.

'Sorry, do you know if the Kamogawa Diner is around here?'

'The Kamogawa Diner?' repeated the delivery driver in his blue-striped uniform, screwing up his face as he sorted through his packages. 'Never heard of it. The address is round here, is it?'

'Yes,' said Tomomi, stroking his moustache as he showed the man the note he'd made of the address. 'East of Higashinotoin on Shomen-dori is what I was told.'

'Ah, I know the place you mean. Second building on the right along here. See where there used to be a sign?' Clutching a large cardboard box, the driver jerked his chin towards a drab, abandoned-looking building. As Tomomi returned the note to his pocket, the driver flashed a smile, then climbed into his truck.

Tomomi walked slowly down the street, then crossed it and stood in front of the building in question. It didn't look anything like a restaurant. A hesitant expression briefly passed across Tomomi's face then, making his mind up, he pushed the aluminium sliding door to one side.

'Hello, welc—'

The woman inside who turned to greet him seemed to freeze mid-sentence.

'Are you serving meals?'

The young woman slowly tilted her head to one side, then peered into the kitchen as if to check with the chef.

'All I can serve you is the set menu, but if that's okay . . .' said the chef, looking out from the kitchen at Tomomi. His neat appearance seemed at odds with the restaurant's shabby exterior.

'Oh, that's fine. A small portion, please.'

Looking relieved, Tomomi made his way to one of the four-seater tables. A newspaper and weekly magazine had been abandoned on its Formica surface. The previous customer must have just left.

Sitting down on one of the red-cushioned chairs, Tomomi took in his surroundings. There were three other tables like his, plus five seats at the counter by the kitchen. Near the entrance was a shelf suspended from the ceiling on which an LCD television sat alongside a miniature Shinto shrine. There were two other customers: a young man at one of the tables, and an older woman at the counter. Both had their backs to Tomomi. From the outside the place had looked a little sketchy, but on the inside it seemed like a perfectly ordinary restaurant. Tomomi unfolded the newspaper.

'Koishi,' called the young man at the table. 'Could you pour me that tea?'

'Sorry, Hiroshi,' cooed Koishi. 'I clean forgot!' She hurried over to the table with a small teapot and filled his cup.

Tomomi couldn't help thinking that the name Koishi

suited the young woman. He wasn't sure which characters it was written with, but assuming the *ko* part meant 'small' and the *ishi* part 'rock', then she had just the petite build and round face to match.

'Curry was a little spicier than usual today, wasn't it?' said Hiroshi, dabbing at his forehead with a white handkerchief. 'My eyes were practically watering! Has Nagare changed the recipe or something?'

'Who knows! Dad's always experimenting. Probably just felt like spicing it up today.'

So the chef was Koishi's father, then. The place must be a family operation. And it sounded like today's 'set menu' was curry?

'Here's your desser— oops, I mean your mizugashi!' said Koishi, bringing a small tray over to the counter.

'That's right,' said the kimono-clad elderly lady sitting there. 'In the West they might call it dessert, but please, in Japanese cuisine the fruit at the end of the meal is known as mizugashi. Oh, this matcha is beautifully brewed. Could you clear all this away so I can enjoy it?' She pointed at a lacquered wooden tray on which various empty dishes were arranged.

'I was just about to!' grumbled Koishi as she removed the tray and wiped the table down with a duster. 'Dad will be glad to see you've polished everything off.'

'Delicious as always, Nagare!' called the lady into the kitchen, half rising from her counter seat.

'Thank you, Tae,' said Nagare, flashing her a smile from the kitchen. 'I'm glad it was to your liking!'

The lady had mentioned Japanese cuisine, so it seemed that whatever she'd had, it hadn't been the super-spicy curry that the other customer had mentioned. Peeping over from behind his newspaper, Tomomi noted the bowl of matcha tea and plate of fruit in front of her.

'But Nagare, I wouldn't use matsutake mushrooms in that chawanmushi,' asserted the lady, who was still half standing. 'I assume you sourced them from Tanba? The aroma is really too strong, and it overpowers the other wonderful flavours you have going on in the savoury custard. You know what they say: less is more. If you're going to use such a delicate stock for your chawanmushi, the only ingredients you should be adding are lily bulbs, kamaboko, and shiitake mushrooms.'

'There's always something, isn't there, Tae!' said Nagare, wincing as he removed his chef's hat. 'Duly noted!'

'I owe you the same as usual, I imagine?' asked Tae, reaching for her purse.

'Yes, that'll be eight thousand yen, please,' replied Koishi matter-of-factly.

'Thank you for the meal.' Tae handed Koishi a ten-thousand-yen note and left the restaurant without waiting for her change. She was taller than she had seemed when sitting down, and the Tatsuta river design on her obi suited her long, straight back. Tomomi watched her leave, a look of blank amazement on his face.

'Very sorry for the wait,' said Nagare, bringing Tomomi's food over on an aluminium tray.

'This . . . is the set menu?' asked Tomomi, goggling at the array of dishes being laid out before him.

'You'll have noticed we don't have menus on the tables. First-time customers always get the set menu. If it's to your liking, then next time you visit we'll whip up whatever you like. Well, I hope you enjoy!' Nagare tucked the tray under his arm and gave a quick bow.

'Erm . . .' said Tomomi as he was walking away.

Nagare turned. 'Yes?'

'This *is* the Kamogawa Diner, isn't it?'

'If you want to call it that.'

'Then where can I find the Kamogawa Detective Agency?'

'That's what you're after, is it? You should have said so when you walked in here!'

Nagare made as if to take away the dishes, but Tomomi stopped him.

'Oh, no, I'll definitely try the food,' he said, reaching for his chopsticks. 'But if I could discuss something with you afterwards . . .'

Fried tofu and mizuna leaves braised in soy sauce.

Simmered herring and aubergine. Lightly pickled turnip. Seasoned egg scrambled with sardine fry. Vinegared mackerel. Taro stem dressed with ground sesame. The miso-glazed fish was probably pomfret, and the steam rising from it indicated that it had just been grilled. Miso soup with onions and potatoes. Tomomi pressed his palms together in a quick gesture of appreciation then, holding the Kiyomizu-ware rice bowl in his left hand, reached for his chopsticks.

This was his first visit to the restaurant, and yet the array of plates in front of him felt somehow nostalgic. Immediately forgetting how full he'd felt on the way here, he began by sampling the egg dish.

The moment Tomomi tasted the dish, he involuntarily closed his eyes. That sweetness of the egg, mingling with the slight bitterness of the tiny sardines. The nutty aroma of the sesame oil . . . it was all just like back in the day. Tomomi leaned forward and, in a slight breach of etiquette, hovered his chopsticks back and forth over the various dishes, contemplating what to eat next.

Eventually he opted for the herring. It broke apart effortlessly between his chopsticks, and was quite strongly flavoured – just the way he liked it. After cleansing his palate with a slice of pickled turnip, he picked up the bowl of miso soup. Ever since childhood, Tomomi had believed that potatoes and onions were the best ingredients for miso soup. The amount of miso was just right, too. Working his way through the dishes, he emptied his bowl of rice in no time at all. Koishi noticed, and chuckled.

'How about some more rice? There's plenty more,' she said, holding out her tray.

'No thanks. I could keep going, but I'll stop myself here.'

Tomomi wiped his moustache with a handkerchief, then covered the rice bowl with his palm.

His belly felt like it was close to bursting. He slightly regretted eating so enthusiastically.

'Glad to see you enjoyed the food,' said Koishi, pouring him some tea from her pot.

'Koishi,' said Nagare, who had appeared and begun clearing the table. 'The gentleman is actually here for the detective service. After he's finished his tea, show him to the back office, would you?'

So Koishi was the detective, then? Tomomi was a little taken aback.

'Oh! Well, you could have told us *that* when you walked in here,' said Koishi as she carefully wiped the table down. She really takes after her father, thought Tomomi to himself, noticing how much her tone and words matched his.

'So, you'll help me track down the dish I'm interested in, will you?' he asked, looking up at Koishi as he sipped his tea.

'Strictly speaking, it's my dad who does the real detective work,' said Koishi, leaning in close. Her small build meant that her face was almost level with the seated Tomomi. 'I'm just the interviewer. Sort of like an interpreter. See, I don't mean to be rude, but the people asking for our services are liable to be a little . . . peculiar. My dad often has a hard time working out what they're after. So my job is to break it all down for him in a way he can understand, and—'

'Koishi, stop chewing his ear off, would you?' called Nagare from the kitchen, cutting her breathless explanation short.

'Thanks for the meal, Nagare,' called Hiroshi towards the kitchen. He had been tapping away at his phone the whole time, but now rose to his feet. 'You know, I actually think you got the spiciness just right.'

'Glad to hear it. Especially from a connoisseur like you, Hiroshi,' replied Nagare, a smile spreading across his face.

'I keep telling you, I'm no connoisseur – I just eat too much.' Hiroshi slapped a five-hundred-yen coin on the table, then slid the restaurant's aluminium door open.

'Drowsy!' shouted Koishi at the tabby cat who had been snoozing in the doorway and was now rubbing himself up against Hiroshi's legs. 'Don't even think about coming in here. Dad'll only boot you out again, anyway!'

'That's right,' said Hiroshi to the cat. 'I'd watch out for that Nagare if I were you!' He gave Drowsy a pat on the head, then began making his way east.

'Hiroshi, we're closed tomorrow, so you'll have to find somewhere else to eat, okay?' called Koishi, somewhat regretfully. Hiroshi half turned and waved a hand in response.

With Tomomi the only remaining customer, the restaurant fell silent. Koishi hurried off to the back office.

Tomomi's phone vibrated in his chest pocket. A new message.

You have half an hour.

Looking at the screen, Tomomi let out a small sigh.

'Shall I show you to the office, then?' asked Nagare, who had emerged from the kitchen and was gesturing for Tomomi to follow him.

'The detective agency is at the back, is it?'

'Oh, agency is a bit of a stretch. We just try to help people find whatever dish it is they're after. Hard to make a living from the restaurant alone these days, you see.'

Nagare opened the door by the kitchen and led him down a long, narrow corridor. Its walls were lined with countless photographs of food.

'Are these all your creations?'

'They're nothing special,' said Nagare, smiling as he turned around. 'I just happen to like cooking food as much as I enjoy eating it.'

'Is this that famous Chinese dish?' asked Tomomi, pointing to a photo halfway down the left-hand wall. 'What's it called again?'

'Oh, that,' said Nagare, coming to a halt. 'Yes, that's

fotiaoqiang – "Buddha Jumps Over the Wall". Smells so good that even Buddhist monks were said to jump over the wall of their monastery for a bite.'

'The ingredients for that must be pretty hard to come by. And – sorry, but at a restaurant like this? Who on earth did you serve it to?'

'My wife, actually,' replied Nagare. 'I'd heard it was a cure-all. Didn't seem to do much in the end, but she did keep saying how delicious it was. So, medical effectiveness aside, I'd say it was worth the effort.' A sad smile had come to his lips. 'This way, please.'

Nagare opened the door in front of them. Tomomi bowed to Nagare, then walked straight in.

He found himself in a small Western-style room, with an area of perhaps ten square metres. Two sofas were positioned on opposite sides of a low table. Seated on the one furthest away from him was Koishi, who had changed into a black suit. Tomomi sat down opposite her.

'Koishi Kamogawa at your service,' she said, greeting him formally this time. 'Would you mind filling in your name, address, age, date of birth, contact details and occupation here?' She placed a grey clipboard on the table.

'Do I have to write everything?' asked Tomomi, gripping the pen as he looked Koishi in the eye.

'Oh, don't worry. We're very good with data protection, plus we have a duty of confidentiality. But if it really bothers you, just go with some made-up name – you know, Taro Yamada or something. Just as long as you give us your actual contact details.' Koishi's tone was matter-of-fact.

After thinking for a moment, Tomomi followed Koishi's advice and wrote 'Taro Yamada', followed by a made-up address, and gave his occupation as a civil servant. Then he wrote his actual age – fifty-eight – and, in the contact details section, the number for his personal mobile.

'Well then, Mr Taro Yamada. Let's get to business. What dish are you looking for?' asked Koishi.

'I'd like you to help me with a certain kind of mackerel sushi.'

'What kind, exactly?' asked Koishi, scribbling away with her pen. 'The refined type they serve at the Izu restaurant? Or something a bit more rough and ready, like you get at Hanaori?'

'Oh no, I'm not after some famous restaurant's sushi. I want the kind I had as a child,' said Tomomi, removing his glasses, a faraway look on his face.

'Mr Yamada, do I know you from somewhere?' asked Koishi, leaning forward and studying Tomomi's face.

'No,' replied Tomomi, looking away and hastily replacing his glasses. 'I don't believe we've met.'

'Well, if you say so. So, tell me about this childhood memory of yours,' said Koishi, pen at the ready.

'It's almost fifty years ago now, so I'm afraid it's all a

little hazy,' said Tomomi, as he began, haltingly, to retrace his memories.

He was born in Mushakoji-cho, west of the Kyoto Imperial Palace, about five kilometres north from the restaurant.

'My father was always in Tokyo – I can't remember him ever being home. It was always just my mother, my little sister and me around the dinner table. We hardly spoke – our meals were quiet, sad affairs. And that wasn't where I ate the mackerel sushi, either.' A melancholy look had come across Tomomi's face.

'Then where did you eat it?' asked Koishi, dropping her voice slightly.

'A ryokan near our house. The Kuwano, it was called.'

'A ryokan? So it was made by a professional cook?' asked Koishi, scrawling something in her notebook.

'Not exactly. It wasn't something they served to guests.'

'If we're talking fifty years ago, then you were only eight, correct?' asked Koishi, a doubtful look on her face. 'I don't mean to contradict you, but are children that age normally able to make distinctions like that? You know, between regular food and the kind you're served at a ryokan?'

'Well, yes, I suppose they might have been serving it at the ryokan too. What I mean was, I wasn't eating it as a paying guest,' explained Tomomi, as though proud of this fact.

'Hmm . . . I'm not quite sure I follow!' said Koishi with a wry smile.

'See, the owner actually lived in part of the ryokan, and I used to play on her veranda. When it got to about three o'clock, she'd always bring me out a snack. Nothing too sugary – it was always baked sweet potatoes, or sticky rice with adzuki beans – just something to keep me going. But what I remember most vividly is her mackerel sushi.'

'So, what was it like, exactly?' asked Koishi, her pen at the ready again.

'This is going to sound a little abstract, but when I try to remember it, the first thing that comes to mind is the word "happiness". If you're after something a little more con-crete, I do remember that she used yellow rice.'

'Yellow rice,' repeated Koishi as she noted this down. 'Anything else?'

'From what I can recall, it wasn't as sweet as people tend to make it these days – it had more of an acidic taste. Almost lemony . . . Oh, and I seem to remember the owner of the ryokan saying something about the Ryukyu Islands being crucial to the flavour.'

'Ryukyu – as in Okinawa? Crucial to the flavour of . . . mackerel sushi?' asked Koishi, mystified.

'As I say, this is all fifty years ago, so I might not be remembering everything correctly,' said Tomomi, as though somewhat discouraged by this reaction.

'Maybe she was from Okinawa, eh?'

'Well, I'm not sure about that. But she always used to say something about a "living torii gate",' said Tomomi, tilting his chin back and staring up at the ceiling.

'A living torii . . . Do they have something like that in Okinawa? This is all getting pretty mysterious!' said Koishi, sighing deeply as she tried sketching a picture in her notebook.

'That's about all I can remember,' said Tomomi, glancing at Koishi's drawing as he settled back into the sofa.

'Okay, I've noted that all down. But I have to say, I'm not sure this'll be enough for Dad to go on . . .' said Koishi, flicking through the pages of her notebook, an uncertain look on her face.

'I trust you'll do your best,' said Tomomi, rising from the sofa.

'I doubt we'll be able to make it just the way you remember it. But we'll have a go at recreating it, and then you can come and try it – how does that sound?'

Tomomi nodded silently in response.

'First of all, we'll need to track down this person you mentioned. Then the ingredients. And we'll need to work out the flavouring . . . Will two weeks be okay? That should give us enough time.' Koishi closed her notebook and looked up.

'Two weeks?' asked Tomomi, staring back at Koishi. 'I

can't wait that long. Can't you do it in one? I'll be in town again next week, you see.'

'Someone's in a hurry! Is there some reason why it has to be a week?'

Tomomi closed his eyes and visualized his jam-packed schedule. If he couldn't eat the sushi the following week, there was no knowing when he'd next be in Kyoto.

'Do I have to tell you that, too?' asked Tomomi, his eyes slowly opening again behind his glasses.

'Oh, no,' said Koishi, hastily dropping her gaze. 'I was just curious.'

'Right. Well, I'm counting on you,' said Tomomi, pressing both hands to the table as he bowed.

'It's all down to my dad, really. But I'll make sure he gives it his best shot.'

'I appreciate it.'

'I don't mean to be rude, Mr Yamamoto, but I have to say this is a pretty odd request. This sushi you're describing doesn't sound very tasty at all! There are plenty of Kyoto restaurants that serve incredible mackerel sushi these days – but all you care about is this weird version of yours.'

'You're still young, aren't you? All you care about is eating the tastiest food you can. Get to my age and you'll realize that nostalgia can be just as vital an ingredient. I want to eat the mackerel sushi that made me so happy back then, that's all. Oh, and by the way,' he added with a wry smile, 'it's Yamada, not Yamamoto.'

'Sorry about that. But I don't know about "young" – I'm well into my thirties! One week, eh . . . Can you give us another day at least? How about next Wednesday? The restaurant is closed then anyway, so it'll be easier to fit you in.'

Today, Tomomi had taken advantage of a rare window of free time to visit, but next week he'd be here on official business. He wouldn't be able to skip out on his duties for long, but he could probably wangle an hour or so if he put his mind to it.

'Okay, Wednesday it is. I'll be here around noon. If there's a problem, please let me know as soon as you can.'

'Dad is usually pretty quick at gauging these things,' said Koishi, her eyes creasing slightly as she smiled. 'He'll know straight away whether it's a complete no-go.'

'I'll pay now. I owe you for the meal, too,' said Tomomi, getting out his wallet.

'We only take payment from satisfied clients, so please, pay for the detective service next week. As for the set menu you had, that'll be one thousand yen.'

'All that . . . for a thousand yen? I feel bad paying so little!' said Tomomi, handing her a one-thousand-yen note.

'Will you be needing a receipt?'

'Oh, no, thank you. Ah – actually, if you could write one

out to Taro Yamada, it'll make for a nice souvenir,' said Tomomi with a grin.

'Shall I call you a taxi?' asked Koishi as she prepared his receipt. 'They can be surprisingly tricky to hail around here.'

'Oh, no. I think I'll wander around a bit before heading back.'

Koishi led him back down the long, narrow corridor to the restaurant, where they found Nagare eating a plate of curry at the counter. He had a newspaper open in front of him, and a grim look on his face. When he saw that Tomomi had returned, he hastily put his spoon down and folded up the newspaper.

'Oh, please – don't mind me,' said Tomomi. His shoulders seemed to stiffen as he spotted the newspaper.

Nagare downed his glass of water. 'Koishi, did you manage to find out what the gentleman is looking for?'

'Oh yes, I found out all about it. The rest is up to you!' replied Koishi, slapping him on the arm hard enough for a satisfying sound to reverberate around the restaurant.

'Hey, go easy, would you?' grumbled Nagare as he rubbed his arm.

'Well, I'll be back in a week. Until then!' said Tomomi with a slight smile. He gave a long bow, then walked out of the restaurant.

'Thank you!' said Koishi, bowing in the direction of his retreating figure. 'We'll see you soon!'

'Koishi, what did he just say?' cut in Nagare. When she rose from her bow, she found him glaring at her. '*A week*? How many times do I have to tell you? We always need at least two weeks to get results!'

'I know, I know, but Mr Yamada asked us to make it a week! You're the one who's always saying a detective's main job is to keep the client happy . . .'

'And you're the one who doesn't know when to keep your mouth shut! Well, you've told him now. What are the details? Please tell me it's something I'll be able to solve in a week.' Nagare snatched Koishi's notebook and opened it up.

'Oh, it'll be no trouble for you, Dad,' said Koishi, thumping Nagare on the back. The sound was even louder this time. 'Three days would probably do it, I reckon!'

'But this sushi he's on about – I have no idea what it could be . . .' said Nagare, a series of deep wrinkles forming on his brow.

'Well, finding out is your forte, isn't it? Come on, Dad, I know you can do it. Ooh – you know what? I feel like curry. After seeing how well it went down with Hiroshi . . .' Koishi skipped off towards the kitchen.

Still seated, Nagare began leafing through the notebook. His expression was growing more and more troubled.

'Wow, this curry *is* good!' said Koishi, beaming over at him from the kitchen. Nagare kept his eyes on the notebook, tracing Koishi's writing with his finger.

'*Yellow sushi rice . . . Lemony . . . Ryukyu Islands . . . the Kuwano ryokan . . . a living torii gate . . .* That's all you got out of him? This is going to be tough.' Nagare closed the notebook, folded his arms, and gazed up at the ceiling.

'Don't worry, Dad,' called Koishi from the kitchen as she started washing up. 'I'm sure you'll solve this one in no time. Oh, by the way – why were you scowling at the newspaper like that just now? Something bad happen?'

'Looks like they're passing that consumption tax hike in ten days or so. Things are tough enough as it is. If the tax goes up any more, every restaurant in Japan will be done for,' said Nagare, throwing the newspaper onto the table.

'Oh, it's terrible isn't it,' said Koishi, stacking plates in the cupboard. 'That prime minister made all sorts of promises when he started out, but now all he seems to do is mumble excuses.'

'The guy comes from a family of politicians. He's probably just doing whatever the people around him tell him to do. Still, I'm hoping he still remembers that thing he said about "sticking to his guns" . . .' said Nagare, staring intently at the photo in the newspaper.

'Well, whatever the politicians are up to, we've got a job to do,' said Koishi, removing her apron. 'I'm off to the bank!'

'You're right. I'm not going to have any brainwaves sitting here twiddling my thumbs. I'll head down to Mushakoji-cho – ask around the neighbourhood and see what I can dig up about that ryokan.' Nagare removed his chef's whites and draped them over the back of the chair.

'Alright then. You'll be back for dinner though, won't you? What are we having? I feel like sushi all of a sudden . . .'

'That'd be a bit extravagant. Oh, I get it – hoping for a meal at Hiroshi's place, are you?'

'Got it in one. Great deductive skills, Dad.'

'Hey, it's no use trying to flatter me. Money's tight right now, so if we go, we're splitting the bill, okay?'

'Alright, you old penny-pincher. Just as long as I get to eat Hiroshi's sushi,' said Koishi, a slight blush rising to her cheeks.

2

It was the height of the autumn foliage season, and Kyoto was heaving with visitors. Even Shomen-dori, the street that ran past the Kamogawa Diner, was even busier than usual, with hordes of tourists making their way between Higashi Honganji temple and the nearby Shosei-en Garden.

'I wonder if that Mr Yamada is actually going to turn up,'

said Koishi, standing in front of the restaurant and bending down to stroke Drowsy.

'You did send him a reminder, right?' said Nagare, anxiously surveying the passing throngs of people.

'Of course! Mr Yamada is just a little busy, it seems. He said he'd be here a bit later than last week.'

'But it's one o'clock already,' said Nagare, shooing the cat away as it tried to curl itself around his legs. 'He was here at twelve on the dot last time.'

'Oh! Is that him?' said Koishi, pointing in the direction of Higashi Honganji temple. 'There, getting out from the taxi.'

Dressed in a dark blue suit, Tomomi strode hastily over to where they were waiting in their chef's whites.

'Sorry I'm late. Did you come out here just to wait for me?'

'Oh, we were just enjoying the sun with Drowsy here. Please, come on in,' said Nagare, sliding the door open.

'I *am* sorry for the rush,' said Tomomi, bowing as he walked into the restaurant.

'You have work to get back to, I imagine? We'll be quick. I'll leave you in Dad's hands,' said Koishi, showing Tomomi to a table. In contrast to his more casual appearance last week, Tomomi did look as though he'd only just slipped away from some engagement.

Nagare sat down at the Formica table opposite Tomomi,

while Koishi disappeared into the kitchen. There was a brief pause before Tomomi broached the reason for his visit.

'Well then, did you manage to find out about that sushi?'

'If we hadn't, we wouldn't have asked you to come,' said Nagare, grinning playfully.

'Thank you for your hard work.'

'I wouldn't thank me yet. I've tried making the mackerel sushi you were after, Mr Yamada, but there's a chance it won't match up to your expectations – in which case, I hope you'll forgive me.'

'I'm well aware of that,' said Tomomi, fixing Nagare with his gaze.

'Koishi,' called Nagare, twisting to face the kitchen, 'cut up the second one from the right, would you? Two-centimetre slices.'

From the kitchen came the sound of a chef's knife – five deliberate thuds, at equal intervals.

'Will tea be fine?' asked Koishi, bringing over a black lacquer tray. On it was the mackerel sushi, arranged on a long, narrow Koimari-ware dish. 'We have sake too.'

'Oh, no, definitely tea. I have work to get back to,' said Tomomi, glancing at the dish in front of him. He fell silent, contemplating the dish with what seemed like intense concentration.

'Please,' said Nagare, gesturing towards the sushi.

Tomomi did as Nagare suggested. As if unable to wait

a moment longer, he briefly pressed his palms together, then brought a slice of sushi to his mouth. Nagare and Koishi were staring at him, carefully studying his mouth and expression.

Tomomi began to chew slowly, as though contemplating the flavour.

There was another lengthy silence.

'No doubt about it. This is it. This is what I was after.'

His eyes seemed to moisten slightly. Tomomi picked up another piece of sushi and opened his mouth.

'Phew!' said Koishi, unable to resist clapping her hands together.

'The colour. The zestiness. That *crunch*. It's perfect. I can only describe it as magic. It's exactly the sushi I had fifty years ago. But you've never even eaten it – how on earth did you . . .' Tomomi set his chopsticks down and sat up straight. 'Please, tell me how you did it!'

'Well, I went through everything you told Koishi last week, one by one. The Kuwano ryokan, the "living torii gate", yellow sushi rice, and the Ryukyu Islands. Those were the four keywords. First, I paid a visit to Mushakoji-cho, where that ryokan used to be. Of course, there's no trace of it now, but I asked one of the locals about it. They told me Kuwano was not a surname, but a place name. But there are dozens of Kuwanos all over Japan. I was at a loss.'

Nagare paused for a sip of tea before continuing.

'The site of the Kuwano ryokan had been turned into a block of apartments. There was an impressive tree in the front garden – a Tosa winter hazel, to be precise. I asked someone about it and was told it had been there since the days of the ryokan. So I wondered if the owner might be from the Tosa region. At the same time, I was still wondering about that name, Kuwano. I knew I'd heard it somewhere. I did some more research and realized that the Kuwano river runs through Nankoku – which is in Tosa. So Kuwano and Tosa *were* connected after all. It was time for a trip.'

Nagare smiled, and a grin rose to Tomomi's lips too.

'Dad always likes to see things for himself,' chipped in Koishi, gazing earnestly at her father.

'I closed the restaurant for the day, and travelled to the Kuwano river in Nankoku to see what I could find. First, I looked for this "living torii gate". I asked some locals if they'd heard of such a thing, and they all told me I must mean the Jiju Shrine. Following their directions, I made my way to a small old shrine – and in front of it, I found what I was looking for. Mr Yamada, may I ask what you were imagining this "living gate" to look like?'

'Well,' said Tomomi frankly, 'you have to remember I was only eight at the time. I suppose I imagined it somehow coming alive at night and wriggling around. You know, something a little . . . supernatural.'

'I had similar thoughts at first. But the gate turned out to be mysterious in quite a different way. Take a look.'

Nagare showed Tomomi a photo he'd taken with his digital camera.

'*That's* the gate?' asked Tomomi, who had taken off his glasses. 'Looks more like a tree to me.' He looked baffled.

'That's right. See how those two cedars have merged together to form a kind of torii? They're called the Kuwano torii cedars. They're a well-known local landmark. Instead of chopping down a tree and using it to make the gate, the locals decided to use a living tree. I was convinced this was the "living torii gate" the ryokan owner had been talking about. So I asked the priest at the shrine to tell me more about it, and that's when I stumbled across the juiciest morsel of intel.'

'Dad is always good with juicy morsels,' said Koishi, a delighted look on her face as she poured Tomomi some more tea.

'The priest told me that he remembered a local woman who went off to run a ryokan in Kyoto. A little west of the shrine was a village called Tosayama Nishikawa, and that turned out to be where the owner of the Kuwano ryokan hailed from. Does the name Haruko Taira ring any bells?'

Nagare looked straight at Tomomi.

'Now that you mention it,' replied Tomomi, nodding

slowly, 'I think the staff at the ryokan used to call her Haru-san . . .'

'After shutting down the ryokan, Haruko went back to her hometown, where sadly she passed away many years ago. But I met a woman there who said she had learned the recipe directly from her. I got her to tell me all about it – and this mackerel sushi here is the result. It's pickled Tosa-style, but the mackerel itself I sourced from Wakasa, seeing as that's where Haruko would have got it from back in those days.'

Nagare gazed at the sushi on the table.

'So she was from Tosa, eh? I was convinced she was either an Okinawan or a Kyotoite.'

Tomomi extracted a grain of rice from his moustache with his fingers, then reached for his third slice of sushi.

'In Tosa, there's a type of sushi called inaka-zushi, where they use the local yuzu fruit to season the rice. They combine it with the usual vinegar, giving the rice a yellow colour. It has quite the unique aroma. Not sure I'd call it lemony, though.'

Koishi had taken a seat next to Nagare and seemed to be appreciating the sushi's aroma.

'What's this?' asked Tomomi, noticing the vegetable that was wedged between the sliced mackerel and vinegared rice. 'It looks like thinly sliced aubergine . . .'

'I only figured this part out right at the end. *That*, Mr Yamada, is the "Ryukyu" you remembered. It turns out that in Tosa, they call this species of taro "ryukyu". Sometimes they cut it into thin slices and place them on top of mackerel sushi – a bit like the use of kombu in the Kyoto version of the same dish. You must have just remembered the word "ryukyu" and assumed she was referring to the islands. But I'm guessing that crunchy texture is bringing back memories.'

'So *that's* what that was all about!' Tomomi munched away at the 'ryukyu', a pensive look on his face.

'I don't mean to pry,' began Nagare hesitantly, 'but can I ask why you were eating sushi at that ryokan in the first place?'

'Mine was a rather sad little family, you see. Father was hardly ever home and my mother was always busy during the day. I never really experienced the kind of warmth most people associate with the word "family". But the ryokan owner was kind. Whenever she saw me moping about in front of my house, she'd invite me over.' Tomomi's eyes glistened, a distant look coming over his face.

'And that was Haruko, eh?'

'I just remembered something. Whenever I was eating the sushi, she'd always ask, "Tasty?" So of course, I'd tell her yes, it's tasty, thank you. But then she'd ask me again: "Tasty?" It was sort of annoying having to repeat myself every time I tried a slice, so eventually I blurted out something like, "I already told you it's tasty!" And, well . . .'

'She flipped?' asked Koishi, leaning in close.

' "You rude little thing," she said. "Sometimes once isn't enough!" She had this scary look on her face. My parents never told me off like that.'

Tomomi's eyes were riveted to the ceiling as he recalled these bygone days. 'Then she turned to me and said something like, "We get used to things too easily. You think something's tasty the first time you eat it, but then you start taking it for granted. Never forget your first impressions." Ah, this sushi is bringing back all sorts of memories.' By now Tomomi was gazing lovingly at the dish in front of him.

'Tell me,' Nagare broke in. 'Do you remember Haruko's motto? The person who taught me how to make the sushi told me about a certain phrase that was always on her lips.'

'Hmm, I can't say I do . . .' said Tomomi. 'As I said, this was fifty years ago.' His phone buzzed in his pocket. Another message.

'Sorry, you're in a rush. Koishi, wrap the leftovers up for him, would you?'

'Sure thing. Mr Yamada, I assume you won't be needing a taxi this week either?'

Tomomi nodded, and Koishi rushed off to the kitchen.

'I'm very sorry to have rushed you like this.'

'The important thing is that we were able to find what you were looking for!' said Nagare, a relieved look on his face. 'It's a weight off my mind, I tell you!'

'I'm just glad I spotted your advert in *Gourmet Monthly*,' said Tomomi, breaking into a smile.

'But that doesn't even give our location, or any contact details!' said Nagare, smiling. 'All it says is *Kamogawa Diner – Kamogawa Detective Agency – We Find Your Food*. People go up and down the Kamogawa river looking for us.'

'Plus you don't even have a sign,' said Tomomi, somehow managing to grin and glower at the same time.

'Oh, if we put a sign up we'd be overwhelmed,' replied Nagare calmly. 'People would go on those silly websites and write all sorts of reviews. No – we do just fine with our regulars.'

'We don't want the place to start filling up with so-called *gourmets* and *experts* and the like!' chipped in Koishi from the kitchen.

'So how did you find us?' said Nagare, looking Tomomi in the eye.

'I asked Akane, the editor-in-chief, about this place. Or rather, forced her to tell me about it.'

'So Akane is an acquaintance of yours?'

'Oh, I wouldn't really say she's an acquaintance . . .' mumbled Tomomi, looking away.

'Well, if you read *Gourmet Monthly*, you must have a pretty keen interest in food.'

'Every issue,' said Tomomi, with a wry smile. 'And it kept bothering me, that bit about *We Find Your Food*.'

'That one-line advert is the only way for anyone to find us,' said Nagare, matching Tomomi's expression.

'Then you could at least add a bit more detail!' Tomomi's face had turned serious again.

'Fate works in mysterious ways.' Nagare fixed Tomomi with his gaze. 'I reckon we always meet the people we're supposed to meet. Which is why you ended up walking through that door.'

'Yes, I suppose it really was fate,' said Tomomi, as though deeply moved.

'People do contact the publisher from time to time. But Akane doesn't normally spill the beans,' said Nagare, eyeing Tomomi curiously.

'I suppose my fixation with this sushi must have won her over. I mean, I've been thinking about it for fifty years. I'm just lucky I had that day off last week . . .'

'It really was an obsession of yours, then,' asked Nagare, his voice tinged with admiration.

'You know, I once dreamed of being a chef like you. Making people happy with my cooking,' replied Tomomi. 'Not that my father would ever have let me,' he added with a self-deprecating look.

'Oh, it's not just chefs who make people happy,' said Nagare with an air of certainty.

'Very true. That's why I chose my current profession – because I wanted to make people happy.'

'Good for you, I say.'

'But in my line of work, we don't always get to give people what they want. In fact, sometimes we try and force something on them which they find downright unappealing.'

'Well, you know what they say: sometimes the bitterest medicine works best.'

'Exactly. The thing is, I only ever thought about it from the perspective of the person administering the medicine. If you want to stay healthy, sometimes you have to swallow a bitter pill – in other words, people should just sort of grin and bear things. I never stopped to think how it might actually feel to be on the receiving end. I decided to remind myself just how important it was to eat something you really like . . .'

'And that was why you went looking for the mackerel sushi from your youth?'

Tomomi answered Nagare's question with a simple nod.

'This has made me see everything much more clearly. Again, sorry for rushing you – but I promise there was a reason for the hurry.'

'Well, that's good to hear,' said Nagare, looking Tomomi right in the eye. 'Serve people the best food you can, and if the leftovers are less appealing, then eat them yourself. That's the way we've always done things here.'

'Sorry for the wait!' said Koishi, arriving with the sushi wrapped up in a paper bag. Tomomi took this as his cue to leave.

'So, how much do I owe you?' he asked, getting his wallet out.

'We let our clients decide what to pay,' replied Koishi. 'Whatever feels right. Just transfer it to this account, please.' She handed him a slip of paper with their payment details.

'Understood,' said Tomomi, sliding it into his wallet. 'I'll take care of it as soon as I get back. With a little bonus for the express service.'

'Travel safely,' said Nagare, seeing Tomomi to the door.

'Thank you,' said Tomomi, stepping outside the restaurant and turning to bow deeply.

'I'm just glad we could help you,' said Koishi, smiling at Nagare's side.

'Well, goodbye then!'

Tomomi began walking, but after a few paces came to a halt and wheeled around to face them.

'I just remembered. That motto of Haruko's you mentioned. *Never lose sight of your ideals.* That was it, wasn't it?'

'Bingo!' said Nagare, giving him a thumbs-up.

Tomomi gave a quick bow, then turned and began walking. The shiny black sedan drew up alongside him.

'Mr Yamada!' called Nagare. Tomomi started and turned around again.

'Please. We're counting on you!'

Nagare bowed his head slightly. Tomomi smiled and nodded, then turned on his heel and carried on walking.

'Mr Yamada seemed very happy with that, didn't he?' said Koishi, turning to face Nagare. 'Great work once again, Dad.' She glanced down at her feet to find Drowsy, who immediately mewed at her.

'Don't underestimate the power of a slice of lowly mackerel sushi,' said Nagare with a sigh. 'That one dish might just have changed the future of the country, Koishi!'

'The . . . country? Dad, you're exaggerating again,' she replied, thumping him on the back. 'Don't get too full of yourself!'

'Never mind, then. Let's just look forward to that bank transfer, eh? Right, time to tuck in to the rest of that sushi!'

'Oh, Dad, I wanted to ask. Why did you make seven rolls of sushi, but only pick one?'

'Well, I was experimenting with the seasoning of the vinegar, the cut of mackerel, and how long to marinate it. The second one from the right ended up tasting best. Just because someone's nostalgic about a certain dish doesn't mean you can get away with some sub-par imitation. If you really want them to say, "Ah, this tastes just like it did back then!" then it has to be truly mouth-watering.'

'Oh, no. Does that mean we're having a load of sub-par sushi for dinner?'

'I meant relatively speaking! I think you'll find they're all pretty delicious, actually. Oh, that reminds me. I picked up some nice sake in Tosa. One's called Suigei, the other Minami. I hear they're pretty special.'

'Brilliant! Nothing like a bit of sake in the afternoon. Still, Dad . . . do you really think we can get through a whole two bottles on our own?' She seemed to be asking his permission for something.

'Well, if it's Hiroshi you're planning on inviting, at least get him to bring a tray of sashimi!'

'How did you know?'

'Oh, it's written all over your face. Anyway, I'm a detective, remember? I don't forget important clues – like the fact that Hiroshi also closes on Wednesdays.'

'Real pro, aren't you!' said Koishi, giving him another thump on the back.

'Just very good at reading what's on my daughter's mind is all.'

'Which is probably why I'm such a heavy drinker.'

'Hey, enough complaining! Come on, help me get ready,' said Nagare, turning towards the altar in the corner. 'We can't keep your mother waiting!'

Chapter 4:
Tonkatsu

1

The long, bitter winter was over, and spring had finally come to Kyoto.

Walking from Higashi Honganji temple, Suyako Hirose crossed the wide avenue of Karasuma-dori and came onto Shomen-dori. The colours of spring – pale blues, lemon yellows, pastel pinks – were also on display in the clothing of people passing down the narrow street.

Meanwhile, making her way east, Suyako was wearing a plain, charcoal-grey dress and black jacket.

She'd done her homework before getting here, so she felt reasonably convinced that the plain-looking building in front of her was her destination. Still, given the absence of any sign or other indications that it was open for business, it was hard to be sure.

By the sliding aluminium door was a small window. The chatter drifting through it certainly sounded like that of a restaurant, while the fragrances wafting out reminded Suyako of the food section of a fancy department store.

'Thanks for the meal!'

The door flew open, and a man in a loose-fitting white jacket strolled out before closing it again. The tabby cat that had been dozing in front of the building rushed over to him.

'Excuse me,' Suyako said to the man, who had started stroking the cat. 'This *is* the Kamogawa Diner, right?'

'Yeah, sounds about right. Mr Kamogawa and his daughter run the place, if that's what you mean,' he replied, then bowed slightly. Suyako gently slid the door open again.

'Here for a meal?' asked Nagare Kamogawa, wiping his hands as he emerged from the kitchen.

'Actually, there's a dish I'd like you to help me find.'

'Well, if it's the detective service you're after, my daughter's the one to talk to,' replied Nagare plainly, looking at Koishi.

'Though it's Dad who does the real detective work,' said Koishi. 'Are you hungry?'

The clock showed half past twelve.

'What kind of food do you serve?' asked Suyako, eyeing the ramen bowl that had been left on the counter, in which a small pool of broth remained. 'I'm afraid I'm a little fussy.'

'We serve all our first-time customers a set menu,' said Nagare, taking over from Koishi. 'Any allergies?'

'Oh – no,' replied Suyako, now glancing around the restaurant. 'But I'm not very keen on meat, or anything too greasy.'

'Well, if you're happy with something light, I can serve you right away.'

'That'd be just fine. I eat like a bird,' said Suyako, a relieved look on her face.

'We actually have a booking tonight for a traditional Japanese banquet. I was just preparing the food. I'll pick you out some dishes!'

Nagare hurried back into the kitchen.

'Please, take a seat,' said Koishi, pulling out one of the red-cushioned chairs.

'This place really is quite peculiar,' said Suyako, looking around the restaurant again. 'You don't have a sign, or even a menu!'

'That's right. You did well to find us,' said Koishi, setting a teacup down in front of Suyako.

'I saw the advert in *Gourmet Monthly*.'

'You mean you worked it out from that single line of text?' said Koishi, pausing as she poured the tea.

'There weren't any contact details, and even when I wrote to the editor she refused to tell me. I told her that in that case I really didn't see the point in the advert, but she refused to budge. So I did a bit of asking around.' Suyako took a long sip of her tea.

'Sorry about that. People are always complaining about that advert, but my dad's a stubborn one,' said Koishi, glancing at the kitchen. 'He always says that, if someone's really destined to walk into this place, that one line will be all they need.'

'Apologies for the wait,' said Nagare, arriving with the food. 'I've prepared a selection of light dishes.' He began removing a series of small plates from the round tray he was carrying and positioning them in front of Suyako.

'Oh, these are adorable,' said Suyako, her eyes sparkling.

'From top left,' began Nagare, tucking the tray under his arm, 'Miyajima oysters, simmered Kurama-style, miso-glazed baked butterburs with millet cake, bracken and bamboo shoot stew, chargrilled moroko, breast of Kyoto-reared chicken with a wasabi dressing, and vinegared Wakasa mackerel wrapped in pickled Shogoin turnip. In the bottom right you have a hamaguri clam broth thickened with kudzu starch. Tonight's customer asked me to create something that evoked both the lingering winter and the onset of spring, which led to the dishes you see here. Today's rice is of the Koshihikari variety, sourced from Tamba. Please – enjoy the meal.'

'I don't even know where to start!' said Suyako, her eyes widening as she reached for her chopsticks.

'I'll leave the teapot here. Just give me a shout if you need a refill!' said Koishi, retreating to the kitchen alongside Nagare.

First, Suyako's chopsticks moved towards the grilled moroko, her eyes drawn to it by the springlike appearance of the dish. Two of the small fish were arranged on an oval Kiseto-ware plate. Suyako found herself recalling that time, three years ago, when she had eaten at a traditional restaurant in Kyoto with her ex-husband, Denjiro Okae.

With a smile creasing his features, he had told her you could catch moroko in Lake Biwa, and that in Kyoto it was seen as a seasonal delicacy that heralded spring. Suyako remembered thinking that Denjiro had become every inch the Kyoto man.

Dipping the fish in the mix of vinegar and soy sauce provided, Suyako polished them off in no time, then tried a mouthful of the mackerel wrapped in pickled turnip. She'd had mackerel sushi many times. In her hometown of Yamaguchi, she'd occasionally finish off a meal at her favourite small restaurant with a Sekisaba mackerel roll. But she'd never had it with something pickled like this. The sweetness of the turnip mingled pleasantly with the sourness of the vinegared mackerel on her tongue.

Next she turned to the bowl of clam broth. She removed the lid, with its maki e design depicting a budding willow tree, and was greeted by a cloud of steam heavy with the fragrance of the clams and their yuzu garnish. Suyako took a sip of the broth, then let out a deep sigh.

'Food to your liking, then?' asked Nagare, returning from the kitchen.

'Oh, it's exquisite,' said Suyako, dabbing at her mouth with a lace handkerchief. 'Almost too good for a country bumpkin like me!'

'Where are you visiting from?'

'Yamaguchi prefecture.'

'That's a long way,' said Nagare, clearing away the plates she'd finished. 'Thanks for making the trip. Once you're finished here, we'll be happy to show you to the office.'

Once Nagare was out of sight, Suyako took the Kurama-style simmered oyster and placed it on top of her rice, then poured some tea over the bowl and began bolting it down. With the occasional pause to sample the wasabi-dressed chicken breast, she emptied the bowl entirely, right down to the last grain of rice.

'More rice?' asked Nagare, who had emerged from the kitchen again and was extending his round tray in her direction.

'I'm fine, thanks. Oh – sorry for eating so rudely!' Her face had turned red, presumably because she was worried Nagare had seen her steeping her rice in tea.

'Oh, there's no such thing as rude or polite when it comes to food,' said Nagare, clearing away her dishes and wiping the table. 'What matters is that you eat it the way you like it.'

'Thank you for the meal,' said Suyako, putting down her chopsticks and pressing her palms together in appreciation.

'Well then, shall I show you to the office?' asked Koishi, who had been waiting for her cue. She opened the door by the counter and began walking down the corridor. Suyako followed shortly behind.

'What are these photos?' asked Suyako, stopping in the middle of the corridor.

'They're all dishes my dad made,' said Koishi, gesturing proudly towards the sea of photos on the walls of the corridor. 'Japanese, Western, Chinese – you name it, he's done it.'

'A jack of all trades, eh? So he doesn't actually specialize in any particular cuisine?'

'Well, yes, I *suppose* you could put it that way,' said Koishi, with a disgruntled pout.

'Did he make these, too?' asked Suyako, sounding surprised as she inspected a particular set of photos.

'Ah, that was when the owner of a kimono shop asked him to create a fugu menu. That platter there is fugu sashimi, on the hob is grilled fugu, and in that clay pot you can see the rice porridge created from the leftovers of a fugu hotpot. Dad is also a licensed fugu chef, you see.'

'I assumed this was just an ordinary restaurant,' said Suyako, smiling as she turned back towards the area where she'd eaten. 'The decor doesn't quite match the quality of the food you serve, does it?'

'Do you like fugu, then?' asked Koishi grumpily as she carried on down the corridor.

'Well, I'm from Yamaguchi,' replied Suyako airily. 'So yes, I've been fond of it since I was a little girl.'

'Lucky you. The first time I ever had it was to celebrate getting into university!' said Koishi over her shoulder.

'My father was a university chancellor, so people often gave it to him as a gift.'

'I see,' said Koishi. Sensing that this bragging was going to continue, she found her expression turning sour, and opened the door at the end of the corridor more noisily than was necessary.

'In here, please.'

Nodding, Suyako made her way into the room and settled on one of the sofas, apparently oblivious to the scowl on Koishi's face.

'Could you fill this out for me, please?' said Koishi, her tone even more businesslike than usual as she held out the clipboard. Placing tea leaves into the pot, she glanced furtively at her client. Suyako scribbled down her details.

'Will that do?'

'Suyako Hirose. Fifty years old – well, you don't look it. Right then, what dish are you looking for?' asked Koishi brusquely.

'Tonkatsu,' replied Suyako, looking straight at Koishi.

'I thought you said you didn't like greasy food or meat?' retorted Koishi in surprise.

'Oh, it's not me who wants to eat it. It's for a . . . certain someone,' said Suyako, a pleading look now in her eyes.

'What sort of tonkatsu?' asked Koishi.

'I don't know. That's why I need your help finding it.'

'Well, yes, but . . . Could you at least be a little more specific?' frowned Koishi.

'I don't know where to start . . .' said Suyako, puckering her lips as she hesitated.

'Oh, start wherever you like,' replied Koishi curtly.

'Have you heard of Demachiyanagi station?'

'Of course I have – like everyone else in Kyoto!' Koishi's cheeks had puffed up.

'Well, there's a temple right by the station.'

Stifling a yawn, Koishi tilted her head to one side. 'A temple? Hmm . . .'

'There used to be a tonkatsu restaurant near there. Katsuden, it was called.'

Koishi nodded silently.

'That's the tonkatsu I'm looking for. The one they used to serve.'

'And that restaurant no longer exists?'

This time it was Suyako who nodded.

'When did it close?'

'About three and a half years ago,' said Suyako, a meek look on her face.

'Well, that's not too long ago, is it?' said Koishi, scribbling away in her notebook. 'Katsuden, you said the place was called? Shouldn't be too hard to find.'

'That's what I thought. I searched online for it, but nothing turned up.' Suyako's expression had clouded over.

'Three and a half years ago, you said? I'd have thought people would have mentioned it online. You know, review sites, blogs, that kind of thing . . .'

'Well, *this* place hasn't even shut down, and there's absolutely nothing about *you* online.'

Koishi's expression relaxed slightly. 'I suppose you're right. Dad and I have a thing about people writing strange reviews. We kept asking not to be listed, but the restaurant still ended up on the websites. That's why we took our sign down and made it look like we'd gone out of business.'

'Seems my husband came to the same conclusion,' said Suyako nonchalantly. 'Though I think he at least bothered to keep the sign and noren curtain outside.'

'Wait. Katsuden was run by your husband?' asked Koishi, leaning forward across the low table. Her eyes had widened with interest.

'Yes,' nodded Suyako. 'More precisely, my ex-husband.'

'In that case, why don't you just ask this . . . ex-husband of yours?' Koishi's cheeks had puffed up again.

'If that was an option, I wouldn't be here, would I?' said Suyako, looking down at the table. 'See, he's the person I want you to make it for.'

'Now you've really lost me,' said Koishi, twiddling her pen between her fingers in frustration. 'Why would you want to do that?'

'I married him twenty-five years ago, when he owned a fugu restaurant in Yamaguchi. Fuguden, he called it. My father didn't approve of the match one bit – in fact, my whole family were opposed.' Suyako paused and reached for her teacup.

'You did say your father was a university chancellor. So, why did the owner of a fugu restaurant suddenly decide to open a tonkatsu place in Kyoto?' asked Koishi, glancing up.

'Someone got poisoned at the restaurant,' said Suyako, then took a long sip of tea.

'Fugu poisoning? But that can be lethal, can't it?' asked Koishi with another frown.

'Yes. In fact, the person in question died.'

'I'm sorry to hear that,' said Koishi in a low voice.

'He was my cousin, actually. He'd always been the headstrong type. Once he'd said he'd do something, there was no changing his mind. He'd caught his own fugu, brought it into the restaurant and demanded they cook it for him. My husband was away at a Fugu association meeting that day. He'd left his sous-chef Mr Masuda in charge.

And it all ended in disaster.' Suyako was biting her lip as she spoke.

'I suppose this Mr Masuda felt like he couldn't refuse that cousin of yours, seeing as he was your husband's family?' said Koishi sympathetically.

'Apparently he did refuse – several times in fact. But it got to the point where my cousin was almost threatening him.'

'What happened to the restaurant?'

'It was a small town, so word got around. There was no choice but to shut the restaurant. And that should have been the end of it, but . . .' Suyako's expression darkened.

'Let me guess. Compensation,' said Koishi, flicking through the pages of her notebook.

'Not really. My cousin's family made their fortune in trade, so they weren't exactly hungry for cash.' Suyako lowered her gaze. 'But the whole affair messed up relations with my family. In the end it was my husband who asked for a divorce.'

'But your cousin was the one who marched in there and demanded they cook it,' said Koishi with a hint of indignation. 'It's not like your husband was to blame, is it?'

'No. But Denjiro has a keener sense of responsibility than most people . . .'

'Denjiro is your ex-husband, then?' said Koishi, making a note.

'Yes. Denjiro Okae,' said Suyako, peering at the notebook.

'Did you really need to get divorced?' asked Koishi, pursing her lips again. 'Couldn't you have left Yamaguchi together?'

'This might sound arrogant, but my family is quite well known in Yamaguchi,' said Suyako, straightening her posture. 'The family name is everything. And I had my piano teaching to think about . . .'

'You're a piano teacher?'

'Oh yes. I've taught everyone, from nursery school kids to students at music colleges preparing for competitions. I had more than a hundred pupils at one point.'

'So you stayed in Yamaguchi after the divorce, while your ex-husband came to Kyoto and opened a tonkatsu restaurant.'

'Actually,' said Suyako coolly, 'it seems he spent the first two years or so after the divorce outside the food industry, roaming around doing various jobs in the Tokyo area. It was only later that he came to Kyoto.'

'Why a tonkatsu restaurant?'

'That I don't know. I do remember him bringing tonkatsu home from his restaurant once, saying he'd cooked it for his staff to eat after work. He'd do that sometimes – bring home whatever he'd made them that day.' Suyako was rocking her head from side to side pensively.

'Oh, I love eating spare food from the restaurant,' said Koishi with a smile. 'We're always doing that here.'

119

'I wasn't so keen,' said Suyako, furrowing her brow. 'Sort of felt like I was being given the leftovers.'

'So, why the sudden request to recreate the tonkatsu from your ex-husband's restaurant? Why not just ask him directly? Because you want him to eat it? I'm struggling to keep up here . . .' Koishi was staring at Suyako with an almost pleading look in her eyes.

'Every year on my birthday, the twenty-fifth of October, he used to send me a little something. But last year nothing came.' Suyako seemed to be choosing her words carefully. 'I was a little concerned, so I got in touch. It turned out he'd been admitted to the Japanese Red Cross Hospital in Higashiyama. When I visited him there, just after the New Year, he was terribly thin. Barely a shadow of his former self. He'd been quite a big man in his prime, you see.'

'Sounds like a pretty serious illness,' said Koishi in a quiet voice. Her pen had stopped moving.

'The doctor gave him three months at most.'

'Three months? But . . . that means there's no time to waste!' cried Koishi, glancing at the calendar on the wall.

'According to the nurses, all he talks about is the tonkatsu at Katsuden. But when I tried asking him about it, he wouldn't say a word. And then I happened to see your advert in *Gourmet Monthly* . . .' Suyako gave a long sigh as she reached the end of her story.

'And he hasn't told the nurses what kind of tonkatsu he means, either?' asked Koishi, with another pleading look.

'Not in detail. They did tell me that when he rambled about it at night, he called out "five mil, three mil". Not that I have the slightest idea what that might mean . . .' Suyako shook her head from side to side.

'*Five mil, three mil?* How mysterious. Well, I think I've got all the details now. I'm sure Dad'll be able to figure this out. I'll make sure he doesn't dawdle!' Koishi closed her notebook and got to her feet.

'Thank you,' said Suyako, rising and bowing.

'All okay?' asked Nagare, folding up his newspaper as the pair returned to the restaurant.

'This one's urgent, Dad,' exclaimed Koishi. 'Start looking for tonkatsu!'

'What? Why?'

'Do you remember a tonkatsu restaurant called Katsuden?'

'Katsuden? It does sound vaguely familiar . . .' said Nagare, frowning slightly.

'A little more enthusiasm would be nice!' huffed Koishi.

'Koishi, listen. If you have something to tell me, you

need to calm down and do it properly. It's always like this with you!'

These words seemed to have their intended effect. Koishi indicated a chair for Suyako, then sat down next to her.

'So, Suyako and her husband got divorced for reasons I won't go into. But now he's seriously ill in hospital!'

Koishi explained the situation, starting from the beginning. As he listened, Nagare kept tilting his head to one side, nodding, and at one point fetched a map of Kyoto from the shelf.

'Oh, Katsuden – I remember that place now. Must have been over a decade ago, but I went there a few times. It was just behind Chotokuji temple, by Demachiyanagi station. Small place, with this big, burly owner who'd stand there frying the tonkatsu in silence.'

Nagare opened up the map.

'That's right,' said Suyako. 'I believe it was very near that temple you mentioned. As for that burly owner you mentioned, well, these days he's . . .'

Suyako took a notebook out of her bag and showed Nagare a photo that was wedged between its pages.

'I can just about recognize him,' said Nagare, staring at the photograph. 'But I do remember him being a lot bigger . . .'

The photo appeared to have been taken in a hospital

ward. Suyako confirmed that the haggard-looking man sitting up in a bed by the window was indeed Denjiro Okae.

'What slender fingers you have,' said Nagare, his eyes drawn to Suyako's hand as she held the photo.

'She's a piano teacher, Dad – of course she has nice fingers. Anyway, there's no time for chit-chat!' said Koishi, an imploring look in her eyes.

'Three months, you said . . .' murmured Nagare, unable to take his eyes away from the photograph.

'If he's lucky,' replied Suyako, her voice becoming faint.

'I see. Two weeks should be enough time to track this dish of yours down. Will you be able to come back a fortnight today?'

'Two weeks, Dad?' squealed Koishi. 'Can't you do it any faster?'

'Two weeks,' replied Nagare brusquely. 'That'll be the absolute minimum if I'm going to find out how the tonkatsu was done at Katsuden and then recreate it.'

Suyako got to her feet and gave him a deep bow.

On her way out of the restaurant, Suyako was accosted by Drowsy, who insisted on curling himself around her legs.

'Hey, Drowsy! Enough of that, okay?' said Koishi.

'Oh, I don't mind,' said Suyako, scooping Drowsy up and handing him over to Koishi. 'I have a cat myself, you see.'

'What's it called?'

'Hanon. You know, after the composer who wrote all those piano studies.' Suyako's face lit up. It was the first proper smile Koishi had seen on it all day.

'You really are a piano teacher through and through, aren't you!' she replied, returning the smile. Suyako began making her way west down the street. Nagare and Koishi bowed in her direction, with Drowsy mewing away at their side.

'Looks like I overestimated you, Dad.'

'What are you on about?' replied Nagare as he flicked through Koishi's notes.

'I was sure you were going to turn around and say something like, "Alright then, give me three days!" Have you forgotten what happened with Mum?' Koishi was giving him a sharp look.

'*Five mil, three mil . . .*' Nagare continued leafing through the notebook as though he couldn't even hear her.

'Dad, are you even listening?' asked Koishi, thumping him on the back.

'Food poisoning alone is enough to ruin a restaurant's

reputation. But when someone dies, that's something else entirely . . .'

'What are you mumbling about?' said Koishi, still glaring at him.

'Koishi, I'm going to Yamaguchi tomorrow. May as well spend the night at Yuda Onsen if I'm going that way. I'll bring you back some of those bean-jam buns. Just promise you'll look after this place, okay?' Nagare shut the notebook and got to his feet.

'Come on, Dad,' said Koishi, with puffed cheeks. 'You could at least get us a fugu hotpot kit.'

'That, Koishi,' said Nagare, 'is the kind of luxury we can't afford.' For once, it was his turn to thump her on the back.

2

News came that the cherries had started to blossom down in Kyushu, but in Kyoto their buds were only just starting to show. This year, like most years, it would be another fortnight or so until they were at their peak.

Still, that hadn't stopped crowds of tourists, eager for their taste of Kyoto in the spring, from descending on the area around Higashi Honganji temple. There was a precious quality to the early evening air.

The junction between Shomen-dori and Karasuma-dori

was busy with vehicles. Suyako, dressed in a cherry-blossom-pink dress and thin white cardigan, was waiting at the pedestrian crossing. Compared to two weeks previously, it wasn't just her outfit that had brightened – her expression, too, seemed more cheerful.

The light turned green, and she began striding east. Soon she had reached the entrance to the restaurant.

'Oh, hello, you. Drowsy, was it?'

She squatted down and petted the cat sprawled by the door. With a soft *miaow*, Drowsy hopped onto her lap.

'Drowsy! Get off. You'll get her clothes dirty!' Koishi had come out to greet her.

'Don't worry. This isn't a special outfit or anything.'

'How's your ex-husband doing?' asked Koishi cautiously.

'Oh, the same,' said Suyako, a faint smile playing about her lips.

'Welcome back!' called Nagare as she entered the restaurant.

'Hello again,' said Suyako, bowing in his direction.

'I've prepared a portion for your ex-husband. But first, please, try it for yourself,' said Nagare, pulling out a chair.

'Thank you,' said Suyako, settling at the table.

'Before you start, there's something I want to tell you. About why your ex-husband opened a tonkatsu place.'

Suyako straightened up in her chair. Nagare went on, his expression humble.

'See, I went and spoke to Mr Masuda, the sous-chef at Fuguden. I had to search pretty hard for him, but eventually I tracked him down to Hakata. After making amends for what he'd done, he opened a small restaurant in the Tenjin neighbourhood. Did you know?'

'No,' replied Suyako, her eyes widening slightly in surprise. 'He came to see me when the fugu restaurant shut down – that was the last time I saw him.'

'Denjiro helped set him up with the place in Hakata. He's still running it today.'

'Denjiro . . . helped him?' repeated Suyako, dropping her voice.

'Apparently, he also told him not to contact him after that – which is probably why you didn't hear about it either. Mr Masuda didn't know anything about Denjiro setting up a tonkatsu restaurant in Kyoto, either.'

Nagare showed her a photo of a small traditional-looking restaurant tucked away at the end of a narrow lane, a noren curtain hanging over the door.

'You went all the way to Hakata?' asked Suyako, bowing her head slightly.

'Dad likes to see things for himself, you see!' chipped in Koishi cheerily.

'When I told him about the tonkatsu restaurant, Mr Masuda said, "Well, that makes sense."'

'*That makes sense?*' repeated Suyako, her voice tense.

'Apparently, Denjiro once told Mr Masuda he wanted to open a tonkatsu restaurant one day. Maybe he was half joking, but it seems he got the idea after you complimented him on his tonkatsu.'

'I complimented him?' Suyako's face had turned blank with surprise.

'Koishi, time to start cooking. Remember how I told you!'

Koishi nodded and headed to the kitchen, while Nagare sat up in his chair.

'Whenever he brought you food he'd cooked for his staff, you'd never say a word about it. You just ate whatever he put in front of you, never commenting on how it tasted. Except, that is, when he brought home tonkatsu. Don't you remember, Suyako?' Nagare was looking straight at her.

'I'm afraid I . . .' said Suyako quietly.

'You said, "I had no idea tonkatsu could taste like this!" Denjiro told Mr Masuda all about it – he was beaming, apparently. And not just the once. Every single time, he'd tell Mr Masuda about it – boasting that if it had gone down that well with you, when you didn't normally go near meat or greasy food, it would probably be a hit with anyone. Mr Masuda sounded awfully nostalgic when he told me all this.'

'I had no idea,' sighed Suyako.

'I think it meant a lot to Denjiro that you enjoyed his tonkatsu so much.'

'I never normally ate fried food, or fried anything myself at home, you see . . .'

'Denjiro really is a chef to the core. Even after he shut the fugu restaurant, it seems he chose to keep making people happy by filling their bellies.'

'I don't even remember saying that about his cooking – and I was the one who said it!' said Suyako, her gaze dropping to the table.

'Chefs always remember when someone enjoys their food,' said Nagare, looking right at her again.

'Almost done here!' said Koishi, appearing from the kitchen.

'Tonkatsu's always best freshly fried. I'll bring it over right away,' said Nagare, getting up in a hurry and setting a tray in front of Suyako. On it were some chopsticks and three small plates.

'Thank you very much,' said Suyako, sitting up in her chair.

'My own memory isn't too reliable, so I got a little help from someone who knew Denjiro well. It should be a pretty close recreation.' Nagare began filling the small plates with different sauces.

'What are those?' asked Suyako, leaning over the plates to sniff them.

'At Katsuden they always served three types of sauce with the meal. From right to left: sweet, spicy, and ponzu. They'd

129

serve six bite-size pieces of tonkatsu, so most customers would dip two in each sauce. I'll tell you more about the recipe for those sauces in a moment.'

'Eat this while it's hot!' said Koishi, placing a round Tachikui-ware plate in front of Suyako. 'It's a little early for dinner, so we haven't served any rice on the side.'

'My, this is all very refined,' said Suyako, gazing at the dish for a moment before placing her hands together in appreciation and reaching for her chopsticks.

Koishi and Nagare retreated to the entrance of the kitchen and peered over at her as she ate.

Suyako dipped her first piece of tonkatsu in the ponzu sauce, then brought it to her mouth. She chewed carefully on it a few times. Then her face broke into a gentle smile.

'Delicious.' The word wasn't addressed to anyone in particular, but seemed to burst from her mouth.

For her second piece, she chose the spicy sauce. This time, before taking a bite, she brought it to her nose, smelled it, and nodded. She ate her third piece with the sweet sauce, then repeated the same order for the other three pieces, alternating them with mouthfuls of the shredded cabbage served on the side until, in no time at all, all six pieces of tonkatsu had disappeared from her plate.

'Thank you.' Suyako set her chopsticks down and joined her hands together again over the round plate. 'That was *exactly* how my husband's tonkatsu tasted.'

Nagare sat down opposite Suyako.

'In the twenty years since we separated, tonkatsu has been my husband's constant companion. It's so delicately cooked . . .' Suyako's gaze was still fixed on the plate in front of her.

'The sauces are quite subtle too, don't you think? As his wife, you must have guessed the secret ingredient right away.'

'Bitter orange?' asked Suyako, looking up.

'That's right. Seems he used Yamaguchi oranges. Boiled them into a jam for the sweet sauce, mixed the rind with red chilli pepper for the spicy one, and squeezed their juice into the ponzu.'

'Never forgot those Yamaguchi flavours, did he?' chipped in Koishi, who was standing at their side.

'This ponzu sauce is like the type you get with fugu sashimi, but it goes well with tonkatsu too!' said Suyako, dipping her little finger in the ponzu and licking it.

'There's a tiny bit of garlic in there,' explained Nagare with a smile. 'You know how fugu sashimi is served with negi onion? I think it's a similar idea.'

'But how did you manage to recreate these sauces so well?' asked Suyako, looking keenly at Nagare.

'Mr Masuda helped me with those. I asked him to remember the tonkatsu he'd eaten after work at the fugu restaurant. Normally, it'd be an ordinary chef who'd cook for the staff, not the master of the restaurant, but Denjiro always insisted on making the tonkatsu himself. After you told him you liked it, he started varying the sauce each time.'

'So that's why . . .' Suyako took the Tachikui-ware plate, now empty, in her hand, and stroked it fondly.

'As you'll have noticed, the tonkatsu at Katsuden had a distinctive batter. It's so soft that you might imagine Denjiro used fresh breadcrumbs rather than the usual dried ones, but then they still have quite a crunch. It turns out he actually sourced his breadcrumbs specially from a local bakery.'

Nagare placed a tray full of breadcrumbs on the table. Suyako wordlessly set her plate down, then tested the texture of the breadcrumbs with a finger.

'The bakery was called Ryujitsudo, not far from Katsuden. He'd place custom orders with them. I went to see the owner and asked him about the tonkatsu at Katsuden.' Nagare paused to take a sip of his tea. 'Soft, but also quite fine-grained. Like I said, almost like fresh breadcrumbs, but slightly drier.'

The breadcrumbs trickled gently through Suyako's fingers.

'Now, these have a roughness of five millimetres. But Denjiro always thought three millimetres was the ideal size. Why? Because that was the version you'd so enjoyed. The finer grain made for a softer texture. But then habitual tonkatsu eaters would expect the rougher feel you'd get from five millimetres. Apparently, this was a recurring topic of debate between him and the bakery's owner.'

Nagare placed some breadcrumbs in the palm of her hand.

'Who knew two millimetres could make such a difference!' said Suyako, a sad look on her face as she traced a
fingertip through the breadcrumbs.

'I've written down the recipe, as close as I could get it.
I've included breadcrumbs in both sizes. As for the pork –
and this part is based on my own memory – I think it was
Yoro pork from Gifu prefecture. The frying oil was probably
a mix of untoasted white sesame and Dutch salad oil.'

Nagare tucked a small stack of lined paper into a clear
plastic file, which he handed to Suyako. Now that he seemed
to have finished, Koishi placed a paper bag on the table.

'I wanted to give you it ready-fried, so your husband
could eat it right away. But Dad said it would be better if
you fried it yourself at home when the time was right. Bit
of extra work for you, I'm afraid. Anyway, the frying oil and
sauces are all in there.'

'Thank you for being so thoughtful. Now, how much do
I owe you?' asked Suyako, reaching into her bag.

'Please,' said Koishi, handing her a slip of paper with their
bank details. 'Just transfer however much you feel like to
this account.'

'Thank you ever so much. I'm sure my husband will be
delighted, too,'. said Suyako, bowing deeply to them both.

'It must all have been very tough for him,' said Nagare,
taking her hand.

'Thank you.' Clasping his hand with both of hers, she squeezed it tightly several times.

Wiping the corner of her eye with her little finger, Koishi slid the door of the restaurant open. Drowsy mewled in response.

'Ah, Drowsy, thank *you* too,' she said, bending down towards him. 'I'll be back, okay?'

'Let us know if he says it doesn't taste right, will you?' said Koishi, still teary-eyed. 'We can always get Dad to make it again!'

'I wish he'd never bothered with fugu. Should have just opened a tonkatsu place in the first place!' said Suyako, biting her lip.

'I'm sure your father would have hated that even more,' said Nagare, a gentle smile spreading across his features. Suyako gave a single, long bow, then set off west down Shomen-dori.

'Mrs Hirose!' called Nagare.

She turned around.

'Make sure you fry it right, okay?'

Suyako gave another deep bow.

'I hope her husband will like the taste,' said Koishi as she cleared the table.

'Me too,' replied Nagare vaguely.

'But couldn't you have made it a little quicker? Suyako must have been sick with worry while she waited. Have you forgotten how it felt when you missed Mum's passing? I mean—'

'Koishi,' interrupted Nagare. He sat down on a chair.

'What?' said Koishi, her lips tightening as she sat down opposite him.

'A dead man can't eat tonkatsu,' said Nagare abruptly.

'What? When did he die?' asked Koishi, her eyes widening.

'I don't know exactly,' said Nagare, casting his gaze down at the table. 'But I think he'd already passed away when she dropped by a fortnight ago.'

'But . . . how can that be?' asked Koishi in an almost accusing tone.

'Didn't you notice anything odd about that photo of him in the ward?'

Koishi tilted her head to one side in silence.

'You could see the grounds of Tofukuji temple out of the window. The leaves looked like they were just starting to turn red.'

Koishi sat up in her chair, a look of astonishment on her face.

'Then it must have been early November at the latest. And three months after that would be . . .'

Koishi counted on her fingers. Her shoulders sagged in dismay.

'She had light burns all over those slender fingers of hers. Must have been from splashes of frying oil. That's not all, either. Did you see how Drowsy wouldn't leave her alone? Well, you know he likes greasy food. Her clothes must have smelled of the oil.'

'You think she'd been frying tonkotsu at home?'

Nagare nodded in response. 'Probably carried out all sorts of experiments. But it was harder to recreate that Katsuden flavour than she'd thought.'

'Oh, right . . .' murmured Koishi.

'I think she really did want to eat that Katsuden tonkatsu with him one last time,' said Nagare, a tender expression on his face. 'You know, sit down with his ashes and tell him how good it tasted. That was what she meant when she told us she wanted him to eat it.'

'So she wasn't exactly lying, then,' said Koishi, nodding.

'You know, I reckon Katsuden could be back in business in time for the Gion festival this summer,' said Nagare, his voice brightening.

'What, you think she'd take up his job? After separating from him more than twenty years ago? No chance. She's hardly going to give up being a piano teacher to run a tonkatsu place!' said Koishi, dismissing Nagare's idea with a laugh.

'Married couples are complicated things, Koishi. Sometimes separating just means you're each able to follow the path you want. Some couples get divorced precisely because of how much they care about each other.'

Nagare slowly got to his feet.

'Married couples, eh?' said Koishi, then shrugged. 'Well, I wouldn't know about those.'

'You can be separated in all sorts of ways, and end up very far away from each other, but the bond between you never breaks. Isn't that right, Kikuko?' said Nagare, heading into the living room. He sat down to face the Buddhist altar, the smile on his face as warm as a ray of spring sunshine.

Chapter 5:
Napolitan Spaghetti

1

Making her way out of Kyoto station and onto Karasuma-dori, Asuka Mizuki looked up at Kyoto Tower, dimly visible through the rain.

Her expression darkening ever so slightly, she hastily opened up her plastic umbrella.

I suppose it *is* the rainy season, she thought to herself – and yet she couldn't help feeling a little disappointed as she gazed up at the sky.

The rain was coming down in sheets, spattering violently up from the pavement. Puddles had formed here and there along Karasuma-dori. Asuka picked her way between them, zig-zagging north up the avenue, until eventually she spotted the blurry outline of Higashi Honganji temple through the rain. Retrieving a notepad from the pocket of her red raincoat, she cradled the handle of her umbrella against her right cheek while she checked the map she'd drawn, then hurried across the pedestrian crossing.

This was Asuka's third time in Kyoto. The first had been with her secondary school, and the second with her grandfather Chichiro. All she could remember from those trips was an endless series of temples and shrines. Now, as she walked east along Shomen-dori, leaving Higashi Honganji behind, she could almost hear her grandfather's gentle voice in her ears.

She frowned as she came to a halt in front of a slightly drab, mortar-coated building. 'This can't be it . . .'

The facade of the two-storey structure was a watery grey. Not only was there no sign, but she couldn't even see a noren curtain to suggest that it was open. Though not entirely convinced, Asuka went ahead and slid the door open.

She was greeted by a young woman in white overalls and jeans, who called out a brusque 'Come in!'

'Is this the Kamogawa Diner?' asked Asuka, glancing around the restaurant's plain interior.

'Well, yes.'

'Does that mean it's also the Kamogawa Detective Agency?'

'Oh, so that's what you're here for! The office is in the back. I'm Koishi Kamogawa, head of the agency.' She bowed to Asuka.

'Asuka Mizuki. There's a certain dish I'm hoping you can help me recreate.' Asuka removed her red raincoat and bowed meekly.

'Please could you take a seat? I'll be right with you.'

Koishi began clearing dishes away and stacking them on her tray. There were no customers in the restaurant, but traces of them were everywhere. Asuka managed to find herself a chair that hadn't been occupied.

'Is she a customer?' asked Nagare, emerging from the kitchen.

'Yes – for the detective agency,' said Koishi, wiping the table down.

'Are you hungry?' said Nagare to Asuka.

'You mean I can eat here too?'

'First-timers get the fixed menu. Will that be alright?'

'I'm not fussy. No allergies, either. I'll eat anything!' said Asuka, getting to her feet and bowing.

'We've got a customer coming in tonight who's asked for a leisurely, indulgent sort of meal. I've made a bit more than I need, so I'll serve you some of that,' said Nagare, then trotted back into the kitchen.

'Where have you come from in this rain?' asked Koishi, carefully wiping down the table in front of Asuka.

'Hamamatsu,' replied Asuka briefly.

'Asuka, was it? So, how did you find out about us?' asked Koishi, pouring tea from her Kiyomizu-ware teapot.

'My parents run a small izakaya, so there's always a copy of *Gourmet Monthly* lying around the house. I always wondered about that single-line advert – you know, the one that says *We Find Your Food*.'

'And that led you all the way here? How on earth did you find us?'

'At first I had no idea where to even look. I tried ringing the publisher. The editor was kind enough to come on the line, and we had a long chat about this and that. Then she agreed to break with protocol and give me a hint. That's how I finally found my way here.'

'An izakaya in Hamamatsu, eh? I bet you serve good eel.'

'Oh, we do eel, but it's our gyoza that people really talk about.' Asuka took a sip of her tea.

'Ah yes – Hamamatsu is a gyoza town, isn't it,' said Nagare, approaching with a tray full of food.

'Yes – in fact, we've overtaken Utsunomiya to become the number one gyoza spot in Japan!' said Asuka, puffing out her chest.

'Eel and gyoza. I can't get enough of either,' said Koishi, placing a crescent-shaped lacquer tray in front of Asuka, together with a pair of Rikyu chopsticks.

Asuka had been expecting something simple – this was supposed to be a casual restaurant after all – and the sight of the elegant tray and chopsticks took her by surprise. She wasn't very used to fancy eating, and yet it seemed she was about to be served some sort of refined Kyoto cuisine.

'I'm afraid I'm not very good with etiquette,' said Asuka, her shoulders slumping.

'Oh, don't worry about manners. Just tuck right in!' said Koishi, spraying mist over the tray.

'Even at a casual place like this, it wouldn't be Kyoto if we didn't pay attention to the seasons. This is all early summer fare. Like Koishi said, just relax and tuck in.'

Asuka watched nervously as Nagare transferred a series of tiny plates, each smaller than the palm of his hand, onto the lacquer tray in front of her.

'These are so pretty!' she found herself blurting out.

'Oh, they're a real mix. Antiques, old Western plates, some by modern artisans . . .'

Soon the tray was a riot of flowery colour. Asuka counted them, pointing to each in turn. Twelve dishes.

'Starting from the top left: thinly sliced Akashi sea bream sashimi, with a prickly ash bud and miso dressing – to be enjoyed with the ponzu dipping sauce. Miso-glazed Kamo aubergine. Maizuru cockles sandwiched between slices of myoga ginger. Gizzard shad marinated in sweet vinegar, served in a miniature sushi roll. Fried matsutake, conger eel grilled two ways, Manganji sweet pepper tempura, abalone pickled in Kyoto-style sweet white miso and then grilled. Fish paste noodles, Kurama-style local chicken, smoked mackerel with a pine nut stuffing. Fresh soy milk curd and vegetables pickled with red perilla. Everything's bite-sized, so it should be nice and easy to eat. I'll bring you some eel-topped rice once that's finished cooking. Please, enjoy the meal!'

With his explanation complete, Nagare tucked the tray under his arm.

'I've never eaten anything like this before. I don't even know where to start!' said Asuka, her eyes sparkling.

'Just eat whatever you fancy, however you fancy,' said Nagare, then bowed and headed back to the kitchen.

'Thank you,' said Asuka, joining her hands together humbly in front of the food. Then she reached for her chopsticks.

Asuka dipped the sea bream in the ponzu and inserted it into her mouth, then let out a little gasp. Next, without a moment's hesitation, she sprinkled some salt on the deep-fried matsutake, took a bite, and nodded vigorously.

Nagare arrived with an earthenware pot, steam issuing from its lid, and set it down on the table. 'Watch out, this is hot!'

'Smells wonderful!' said Asuka, her nose twitching away.

'Freshwater eel is tasty enough, but there's something about the lightness of saltwater anago. The rice is topped with grilled anago from Akashi, with a garnish of green peppercorns.' Nagare removed the lid from the pot, unleashing a thick column of steam.

Napolitan Spaghetti

As Asuka tucked in to the eel rice, a glowing smile spread across her face. Nagare, watching, bowed in her direction.

By the fourth dish, Asuka's eyes appeared to be moist with tears. By the fifth, they had begun to trickle down her cheeks, and by the seventh she was fully weeping. She kept dabbing at her eyes with her handkerchief.

Koishi, feeling like she couldn't just stand there, leaned over. 'Are you okay? Feeling out of sorts?'

'I'm sorry,' replied Asuka, smiling through her tears. 'It's just so . . . good. Whenever I eat delicious food, I always seem to start crying.'

'Well, as long as you're okay . . .' Koishi cleared the empty dishes and ducked back under the curtain into the kitchen. Nagare had been observing the whole scene.

Asuka gazed at the five dishes remaining in front of her. She'd come here to get help with a dish from her past, but now she couldn't help thinking that maybe that was just destiny's way of bringing this food into her life. It really had moved her deeply. Lovingly, and almost reluctantly, she finished off the remaining plates.

'How was that, then?' asked Nagare, appearing by her side as soon as she set her chopsticks down.

'Thank you. Delicious doesn't even cover it. My heart is all aflutter!' Asuka put a hand to her chest and took a deep breath.

'Glad to hear it. Koishi is getting ready in the office, so if you could just wait a moment . . . I'll bring you some hot hojicha.'

Nagare cleared away the empty dishes, then replaced her teapot with a Banko-ware one, alongside which he positioned a fresh teacup.

The restaurant had fallen silent, and the only sound that could be heard was that of Asuka sipping on the roasted green tea. After each sip, she'd let out a little sigh. She repeated this process several times.

'Sorry for the wait,' said Nagare, reappearing at her side.

'Not at all,' said Asuka, getting to her feet.

Nagare showed her to the back of the restaurant and down the long corridor that led to the office.

'What are all these?' asked Asuka, her gaze taking in the photos that lined the walls of the corridor.

'Most of them are just dishes I made,' said Nagare, smiling bashfully as he came to a halt.

'Is this your wife?' Asuka pointed to a woman sipping from a glass in the shade of a birch tree.

'That was the last photo I took of her. We were in Karuizawa. Ate her favourite soba in Nagano, went back to her favourite hotel, and drank her favourite wine. Looks like she's on cloud nine, wouldn't you say?'

It might just have been Asuka's imagination, but Nagare's

146

eyes seemed to glisten slightly. Not quite knowing what to say, she ended up silently following him as he led her on down the corridor.

'Asuka Mizuki. Sounds like a stage name or something!' said Koishi, watching her client scribble down her details in her girly, rounded handwriting. She was sitting on the other side of the low table in the office.

'I always found it a little embarrassing,' replied Asuka, shrugging as she perched on the edge of the sofa.

'Second year student at Shinshu Women's University . . . You're nineteen, eh? The prime of your youth!' said Koishi enviously.

'It doesn't really feel like that,' said Asuka, a hint of despondency in her voice.

'Well then, what's this dish you'd like us to recreate?' asked Koishi, opening her notebook.

'It's some spaghetti I ate with my grandad.'

'What kind?' asked Koishi, scribbling away.

'I think it was Napolitan – you know, Japanese-style tomato spaghetti, with a ketchup and frankfurter sauce.'

'Oh, that's one of Dad's specialities. Did your grandfather make it for you?'

'No. I don't remember him ever cooking for me. We must have had it on one of our trips.'

'Took you travelling, did he? How nice!'

'My parents were always rushed off their feet with work, so it was my grandad who looked after me.' Asuka broke into a smile.

'What was his name?'

'Chichiro Mizuki,' answered Asuka, straightening her posture.

'What about your grandmother?'

'She died from illness not long after I was born,' replied Asuka, her voice turning glum. 'I can barely remember her.'

'And where did you go on this trip with the spaghetti?' asked Koishi, pen at the ready.

'Oh, Grandad took me to all sorts of places. I have no idea where it might have been.'

'Not even the region?'

Asuka silently shook her head. 'Grandad's been suffering from dementia for the past three years . . . It was all so sudden. I never got round to asking him about the trips we went on.'

'I see. I'm afraid this isn't much to go on . . . There must be thousands and thousands of restaurants serving Napolitan spaghetti in Japan,' said Koishi, sighing and looking up at the ceiling.

'I'm sorry,' said Asuka, shyly bowing her head. 'I was only five at the time, you see . . .'

'How about trying to recall what kind of trip it was? There must be something you remember – how you got around, for example. Or maybe something you saw?' Koishi spoke as though addressing a child.

'We stayed in a hotel near the sea,' said Asuka, her eyes squeezing shut with the effort of remembering.

'*Near the sea* . . . Anything else?' asked Koishi, her pen hovering above the page.

'The next day, we took a boat. Actually, I think we drove onto it in a car,' said Asuka, her eyes gleaming.

'A ferry, then,' said Koishi, underlining something she'd written.

'The weird thing is, I'm pretty sure we took the bullet train home,' said Asuka, a doubtful expression crossing her face. 'That's the one part I remember clearly – taking the bullet train back to Hamamatsu.'

'Could you have just rented a car somewhere along the way? My dad always does that.'

'Yes, that's probably it,' nodded Asuka assertively. 'I don't think it was my grandad's car, anyway.'

'What about this hotel near the sea, then? What sort of place was it?'

'Hmm . . .' Asuka seemed to be trying desperately to make sense of her scattered memories.

'How long were you on the ferry?' said Koishi, changing tack.

The Kamogawa Food Detectives

'I feel like it was quite a short trip. An hour or two, maybe?'

'*Short ferry trip* . . .' said Koishi, scribbling away again.

'And before we got to the hotel . . . I remember there were all these bright lights,' said Asuka, half lost in contemplation as she pieced together her thoughts.

'Ah. Some kind of display, maybe?' said Koishi, leaning forward excitedly. But Asuka just tilted her head doubtfully.

'Let's leave the trip to one side for a moment, and talk about this spaghetti. Now, do you remember what the restaurant was like? Or how it tasted?'

'Well, like I said, it was Napolitan-style spaghetti. With a ketchup-based sauce. And sliced frankfurters.'

'Just your standard Napolitan spaghetti, then,' murmured Koishi, crestfallen.

'Wait. It was yellow!' cried Asuka, slapping her thigh.

'Yellow? But isn't Napolitan sauce normally red?'

'I think it was a mix of yellow and red . . .' Asuka stared up at a point on the ceiling, slowly tugging on the threads of her memory.

'Never heard of anything like that . . .' said Koishi doubtfully, as she began sketching an illustration in the notebook.

'Maybe I'm remembering it wrong,' said Asuka, her voice dropping as she seemed to lose confidence.

'What about the restaurant itself – do you remember where it was? What it was called, or what sort of place it was?

I guess that's asking a lot of a five-year-old . . .' Even as she posed her questions, Koishi sounded like she'd half given up.

'We got to the station, then Grandad took me by the hand. I think we walked for quite a while.' Asuka seemed to be recalling the warmth of Chichiro's hand.

'*Walked for a while from the station*. Right. And did you walk back there after the meal?' asked Koishi, gripping her pen.

'We had the spaghetti, then got on the bullet train and went home. I think I was crying all the way.'

'Tired, were you?' asked Koishi with a grin.

'I think so. But more than that, it was the spaghetti. It was just so . . . delicious, you see . . .'

'Ah, of course. You start crying whenever you eat something tasty.'

'I think it was that spaghetti that started it, actually.' A faraway look had come over Asuka's face. 'I think that's all I can remember . . . Oh, I think I burned my mouth. That, and . . . a big red bottle, which Grandad took a photo of.'

Koishi jotted down everything Asuka had mumbled, then looked up at her. 'If your grandfather took photos on the trip, why don't you just look at them? Have you tried digging them out?'

'One of the first signs of Grandad's dementia was that he started throwing things away at random. You know – his bankbook, his registered seal, even wads of cash. Shoved them all in a bin bag and chucked them out with the rubbish. His photos were in there, too . . .' Asuka's voice had dropped to a murmur.

'I'm sorry to hear that.'

'He used to live with me and my parents, but then he started throwing away all sorts of important things. That's why he's been in a home for the past couple of years.'

Asuka thought back to the happy days the four of them had shared. Her grandfather had been the type of drinker who got merrier and merrier the more he drank. Before he went to bed, he'd always give her a gentle pat or two on the head.

'I guess if the photos were still around you wouldn't have needed our help. Well, we'll just have to try. I reckon Dad'll track this spaghetti of yours down somehow – he always does!' Koishi closed her notebook.

'Thank you for your help,' said Asuka, sitting up and then bowing deeply.

'Tell me – what made you curious about this spaghetti all of a sudden?'

'Well, firstly, I want to eat it again. But more importantly, I want my grandad to eat it. If I can, I want to take him back to the same restaurant.'

'Right.'

'But he barely even knows who I am these days,' said Asuka, her gaze dropping to the table.

'We'll just have to serve him some of that spaghetti then, won't we! Leave it to us, okay?' said Koishi, putting a hand to her chest.

'Did you find out what she's after, then?' asked Nagare, folding up the newspaper that he'd been reading at the counter.

'I'm afraid my memory is a bit useless,' cut in Asuka.

'Napolitan spaghetti,' said Koishi. 'One of your specialities, isn't it, Dad?'

'I'm guessing my own recipe won't quite hit the spot?' asked Nagare with a grin.

'Oh, as long as it's tasty, I won't mind,' said Asuka, returning his smile.

Nagare turned to Koishi. 'Did you make arrangements for her next visit?'

'Oops – slipped my mind completely. How's two weeks today?'

'That's fine,' nodded Asuka, as she made her way out of the restaurant.

'Staying the night in Kyoto, are you?' asked Nagare, eyeing the large bag that Asuka had shouldered.

'I was planning to, but it's supposed to rain all day tomorrow too. I think I'll just head back to Hamamatsu.'

'Kyoto can be nice in the rain, you know,' said Nagare, looking up at the dark grey sky.

'I'll save it for next time,' smiled Asuka.

'We'll do our absolute best to find this dish of yours,' said Nagare, fixing Asuka with his gaze.

'I'll be looking forward to it!'

Asuka bowed and walked off in the direction of Higashi Honganji. After seeing her off, Nagare and Koishi headed back inside the restaurant.

'These rainy days just keep coming, don't they? Getting a little sick of them, to be honest,' said Nagare, sitting down on one of the red chairs.

'I wonder if this'll be enough for you to go on . . .' said Koishi, sitting down beside him and opening up her notebook.

'Won't know until we try, will we?' said Nagare, getting out his reading glasses and scanning through her notes.

'It's all so vague!' said Koishi, looking over his shoulder. 'I mean, you can get Napolitan spaghetti pretty much anywhere . . .'

'A hotel near the sea, and a ferry, eh?' said Nagare as he thumbed through the pages. Then, in a quiet murmur: 'And what's this? *Bright lights.* Hmm . . .'

'I guess this one's going to be a bit of a stretch, even for you, Dad. I mean—'

'I'll set off tomorrow,' interrupted Nagare.

'What? You mean you already know where you're going?' asked Koishi in an excited voice.

'I have a pretty good idea what sort of trip they went on. But I'm not so sure about this restaurant she mentioned . . .' said Nagare, folding his arms.

'Oh. For a moment, I thought you'd cracked it already . . .' said Koishi, her disappointment showing in her voice.

2

'Rain again,' muttered Asuka, shrugging slightly as she made her way out of Kyoto station and onto Karasuma-dori.

The rainy season hadn't ended yet, she reminded herself as she made her way north up the avenue. This sort of dreary weather was only to be expected.

The rain pattered louder and louder on her umbrella. As she waited by the pedestrian crossing, raindrops splashed mercilessly onto her feet. When she arrived in front of the Kamogawa Diner, Asuka folded up her umbrella and took a long, deep breath.

'Welcome!' called Koishi, sliding open the door. 'More rain, eh!'

'Hello again,' said Asuka, removing her red raincoat and hanging it from a hook on the wall.

It was after lunchtime, and it seemed the restaurant's customers had already departed. The place was empty, but there were traces of various meals still on the tables. It had been the same last time: no one in sight, and yet a feeling of human warmth filled the space. Asuka thought to herself, not for the first time, that this really was quite an unusual restaurant.

'Here you go,' said Koishi, holding out a towel.

'Thanks.' Asuka began patting her tights dry.

'You must be hungry,' said Nagare, removing his chef's hat as he emerged from the kitchen. 'It'll be ready in just a minute!'

'Wonderful,' said Asuka with a bow. When she looked back up, Nagare flashed her a smile, then returned to the kitchen. Asuka handed the towel back to Koishi, then took a seat.

'How's your grandfather doing, then?' asked Koishi, pouring some tea from her Kiyomizu-ware teapot.

'I went to see him the day before yesterday. But he still doesn't seem to recognize me . . .' A shadow crept over Asuka's face.

'That must be really tough,' said Koishi, a glum look coming over her own features.

The clanging of a frying pan came from the kitchen, and

an appetizing smell began to waft into the room. Gathering herself, Koishi placed a pink mat in front of Asuka, along with a fork.

'Koishi, it's almost ready,' called Nagare from the kitchen. 'Help her with the apron, would you?'

'Can't have your clothes getting stained, can we!' said Koishi, placing a white apron over Asuka's beige dress and tying the straps at the back of her neck. Asuka felt slightly bewildered by what was about to happen.

'Here we are!' said Nagare, hurrying over with a silver tray in his hands. 'The sauce will splatter, so watch out!' On the mat in front of her, he placed a wooden dish on top of which was a round griddle dish that was hissing and crackling away. Asuka instinctively arched away from the plate.

'Please, tuck in while it's hot. But watch you don't burn your mouth this time,' smiled Nagare, standing at her side.

'But this is . . .' Asuka's eyes had opened wide.

'Is it all coming back? If I'm not mistaken, this is the spaghetti you had with your grandad that time. Please, enjoy!' Nagare placed a small bottle of Tabasco on the table, tucked the silver tray under one arm, and headed back to the kitchen.

'Here's some chilled water!' said Koishi, setting a glass and pitcher down on the table before following Nagare into the kitchen.

On the sizzling griddle dish was a mound of spaghetti

coated in a red tomato sauce. But the rest of the plate's surface was covered by a layer of whisked egg, so that the other dominant colour was yellow. Three frankfurters, split down the middle, adorned the mound of spaghetti. Asuka joined her hands together, then hastily reached for her fork.

'Agh!' she winced as she thrust the first mouthful of spaghetti into her mouth.

The pasta that was steaming away on the hot plate in front of her was incomparably hotter than regular spaghetti. She was probably going to burn the inside of her mouth, but it was just too delicious, and she simply couldn't bear the idea of waiting for it to cool.

'Mmm . . .' she murmured as she twisted the spaghetti onto her fork.

She tried one of the frankfurters. There was a satisfying crunch as she bit into it and its skin burst. Meanwhile, the egg was cooking away on the plate, getting firmer and firmer. Asuka worked some of it into a forkful of spaghetti, then inserted the whole thing into her mouth.

'What a combination!' she said to herself. Tears were running down her cheeks.

Her thoughts turned to memories of her grandfather. Her primary school entrance ceremony – and after that, middle and high school, too. He'd always been the one who was there for her – not her mother or father, but Chichiro. Her grandfather.

'Looks like we got it right, then?' asked Nagare, emerging from the kitchen.

'Yep,' Asuka replied simply as she dabbed at her cheeks with a handkerchief.

'Apparently, they don't actually call it Napolitan at the restaurant in question. They just call it "Italian". It's a place called Chef, in Nagoya. Although they're actually more known for their ankake spaghetti.'

'So we ate it in . . . Nagoya?' Asuka seemed surprised by the location.

'Yes. I think your trip looked something like this,' said Nagare, opening up a map on the table while Asuka and Koishi peered over.

'I reckon you were heading for Toba, in Mie prefecture. Your grandfather was probably taking you to the aquarium there. Kids love that place. And if you stayed at a hotel by the sea, then took a ferry the next day, then your route would have been something like this . . .' Nagare drew a red line across the map.

'We stayed the night in Irago?' asked Asuka, in a curious voice.

'I reckon those bright lights you remember were from a denshogiku farm.'

'Den-sho-giku?' repeated Asuka and Koishi in unison.

'It's a special way of growing chrysanthemums. That area – the Atsumi peninsula – is famous for it. They grow the plants in a greenhouse, and keep the lights on nice and bright all night long. That way, they can control when they blossom.' Nagare got out a tablet and started swiping through a series of photos. 'They look quite special at night, don't they!'

'So that's what I was remembering?' asked Asuka, a little doubtfully.

'You must have set off quite late, for whatever reason. Your grandfather wanted to take you for a ferry ride. I reckon you rented a car at Toyohashi, then spent the night in Irago. The next morning you took the ferry to Toba. You spent the day there, then drove back around the peninsula to Nagoya. That seems to have been your itinerary.'

'Hmm, denshogiku . . . Now that you mention it, I feel like we learned about that in school!' said Koishi, nodding as she folded her arms.

'Driving north from Toba along the Ise Bay would take you to Nagoya. You dropped the rental car off there and took the bullet train back to Hamamatsu. But before that, you stopped by that restaurant. I'm sure your grandfather couldn't resist the chance to enjoy a good meal. Finishing the trip with a plate of spaghetti at Chef was probably something he'd been planning from the start. It's the kind of thing he knew a kid would enjoy. I bet he couldn't wait for you to try it.'

Nagare continued swiping through his photos, until he found one of the restaurant in question.

'That's the place, is it?' said Asuka, her voice filling with emotion as a smile spread across her face.

'Apparently lots of people like to make a deliberately long stopover in Nagoya, just so they can visit this restaurant. What they call "Italian" in Nagoya isn't quite the same as the usual Napolitan. You pour some whisked egg onto a hot plate, then add the spaghetti on top. That yellow colour you remember must have been the egg. As for the red bottle that your grandfather took a photo of,' said Nagare, swiping through the photos on the tablet, 'that must have been this. A huge bottle of Tabasco. I couldn't help snapping a photo of it myself.'

'Tabasco!' exclaimed Asuka, picking up the small bottle of sauce on the table and comparing it with the one in the photo. Then, fork back in hand, she polished off the rest of her meal, scraping up all the egg that had stuck to the griddle dish and devouring it along with every remaining strand of spaghetti.

When she was done, she gazed at the now-empty dish for a moment, before joining her palms together and thanking Nagare for the meal.

'How old is your grandfather now?' asked Nagare, who had been watching her finish the meal.

'He turned seventy-five last month,' replied Asuka.

'Still young, isn't he! Well, I hope this spaghetti triggers some memories.'

'I hope so too . . .' said Asuka in a quiet voice.

At Nagare's signal, Koishi set a paper bag down on the table.

'Of course, taking him to the restaurant would be ideal,' said Nagare. 'But if that's not possible, you'll have to cook it for him yourself. I've prepared a set of ingredients together with a griddle dish. I don't know if you can really call it a recipe, but I've written down some instructions, too.'

Asuka smiled for a moment. Then, with what seemed like sudden resolve, she sprang to her feet and bowed deeply to Koishi and Nagare.

'Thank you so much, really. How should I pay?' she asked, getting her purse out of her bag.

'However much you think it was worth. Please just transfer it to this account,' said Koishi, handing her a slip of paper.

'Got it. I'll do it as soon as I get home.'

'You're still a student, aren't you? Don't go overboard. A little will be just fine!' said Koishi, smiling at her.

'Thanks. I appreciate it.' Asuka bowed again to them both, pulled on her red raincoat, and opened the sliding door.

'Oh, Drowsy, you really can't come in here!' said Koishi, chiding the tabby who was poking a foot through the door.

'Poor thing, sitting out here in the rain. What's its name?' asked Asuka, squatting to pet the cat.

'Drowsy,' said Koishi, crouching by her side. 'Always lying around with his eyes half-closed, you see.'

'Looks like the rain has passed, eh?' said Nagare, holding out a palm towards the sky. Weak sunlight was filtering through the clouds.

'Can I ask you something?' said Asuka, looking Nagare in the eye as she stood up.

'Of course,' said Nagare, returning her gaze.

'Why do you think I remember that spaghetti in particular, out of all the other dishes I ate with Grandad?'

'Well, this is just a guess, but . . .' Nagare paused and took a breath. 'I wonder if this trip was the first time your grandfather treated you like a grown-up.'

Asuka's eyes widened in surprise.

'Until then, you'd probably always just been given whatever everyone else was having. But this trip marked the beginning of your life as an individual, and that plate of spaghetti was the proof. Your own meal, all to yourself – right there in front of you. You must have been over the moon.'

Asuka simply gaped at him, seemingly lost for words.

'That was probably also why you started crying whenever you ate something delicious. Your grandfather must have taught you that eating good food wasn't just about enjoying it, but also being grateful for it. That lesson must have lingered somewhere deep in your memory.'

By now, Asuka's eyes were wet with tears.

'Say hello to him from us,' said Koishi with a grin.

'Thank you so much.' Asuka gave another deep bow, then set off. Nagare and Koishi watched from behind as she made her way down the street.

'Classy detective work, Dad,' said Koishi as they walked back into the restaurant. 'I should never have doubted you!'

'Must have been a pretty fun trip for a five-year-old. Lucky parents, having someone like that to help raise their kid!'

'I never got to go anywhere with *my* grandad.' Koishi had stopped clearing the table and was staring into space.

'He was even more of a workaholic than I am,' said Nagare, making his way into the living room. 'And if we complained, he'd always launch into one of his lectures about what it meant to be a police officer. I never went on any trips with him either, you know.'

'Come to think of it, I've hardly been on any trips with *you* either, Dad. It was always just me and Mum.'

'*A policeman is always on duty.* That's what he always told me, and that's probably why I was never at home much either – until your mother passed away, that is.' Nagare sat down in front of the altar.

'Left it all to her. Had a pretty hard time of it, didn't you, Mum?' said Koishi, sitting alongside him and praying to the altar. 'Disneyland, the zoo, the beach, hiking . . . It was always just the two of us. But I didn't mind one bit. I always had a great time!'

Nagare lit an incense stick in front of the altar, then got to his feet. 'Fancy going out for pasta tonight?'

'Actually, I'm in the mood for your Napolitan. You haven't made it for a while, you know . . .' said Koishi, an imploring look in her eyes.

'With pleasure. Right then!' Nagare rolled up his sleeves. 'What do you say we make it an "Italian"? I've got those griddle dishes.'

'I thought you gave them to Asuka?' asked Koishi, getting to her feet.

'They came as a set of five. Two for her means three left over. What do you say we invite Hiroshi to join us?'

'Ooh, please. I'll get us some wine that'll pair well with the spaghetti!' said Koishi, taking off her apron.

'Don't go breaking the bank. Tonight's more about quantity than quality! You know, I reckon Kikuko probably fancies a drink too.'

Nagare handed Koishi his wallet, then turned back to face the altar.

Chapter 6:

Nikujaga

1

Spring and autumn are when the biggest crowds descend on Kyoto. In particular, spring sees a rush of tourists all trying to enjoy the short-lived cherry blossom season, leaving some parts of the city literally swarming with people.

It was early afternoon, and the courtyard in front of Higashi Honganji temple was filled with visitors gaping up at the cherry blossom trees, snapping away with their phone cameras.

What was the point of just taking a photo of some isolated cherry blossoms? That was the question troubling the young man in a suit who, as he passed, shook his head from side to side in confusion.

After a lengthy photo session, the crowd drifted towards Shosei en Garden, one of the quieter cherry blossom viewing spots. As though borne along by the flood of tourists, the young man made his way east along Shomen-dori, a map in one hand. Soon enough, he had found his way to the building on the right-hand side of the street that he was looking for.

'This place?' he muttered, glancing alternately at the mortar-coated two-storey building in front of him and the hand-drawn map he was holding. Through the half-open window he was able to catch of a glimpse of the interior.

An elderly lady was sitting at the table, seemingly lingering over her meal. The man wearing whites at her side must be the chef, he thought. There were no other customers inside.

'Hello there. I'm looking for Nagare Kamogawa.'

'You're speaking to him,' said Nagare, turning around and taking in the man's appearance. He was wearing a well-tailored navy pinstripe suit, with a large Bottega Veneta pouch under his arm. His pointed brown boots had an enamel-like sheen.

'Ah. Nice to meet you.' The man walked into the restaurant and glanced at the plate in front of the elderly lady before removing his jacket and hanging it on the back of a chair. 'Oh, is that wild vegetable tempura? Looks delicious.'

'And . . . who are you?' asked Koishi, eyeing him dubiously. She was wearing a white shirt and dark jeans underneath a black sommelier apron.

'Ah yes, where are my manners. Hisahiko Tsuda. I'm here on Akane's recommendation.' He courteously held out a business card.

'Ah, Mr Tsuda. Akane told me about you. I wondered when we'd be seeing you. Hmm, Tsuda Enterprises, eh?' asked Nagare, studying the card.

'And you must be Koishi. I've heard a lot about you from Akane. She told me to look out for a pretty young woman!' said Hisahiko, giving her a meaningful look.

'Young?' said Koishi, blushing. 'More like middle-aged. Isn't that right, Tae?' She patted Tae on the back.

'Koishi, can't you see I'm eating? I'd like to enjoy my meal in peace, if you don't mind!' snapped the older woman. She was wearing a wisteria-coloured kimono, a greenish-grey obi around her waist.

'I'm sorry for the interruption,' said Hisahiko, bowing deeply. 'I just couldn't help myself, what with that delicious-looking tempura you're eating, and this beautiful young woman standing here . . .'

'That sort of smooth talk will get you nowhere in Kyoto, you know,' said Tae, reaching out with her chopsticks and dabbing a piece of ostrich-fern tempura into the dish of thin dipping sauce.

'Are you hungry?' intervened Nagare.

'I feel bad, turning up like this out of the blue. But yes,

if I could get something to eat . . .' said Hisahiko, putting a hand to his stomach.

'We normally serve first-time customers a set menu. Will that be okay?'

'Yes, please.'

Nagare set Hisahiko's card down on the table, then ducked under the curtain separating the restaurant from the kitchen.

'Please, take a seat!' said Koishi, pulling out one of the red-cushioned chairs.

'No sign, or even a menu . . .' said Hisahiko, glancing around as he sat down. 'Akane did tell me about this place, but it's even stranger than I was expecting.'

'How do you know Akane, then?' asked Koishi, placing a teacup in front of him.

'We've acquired the entire magazine that Akane edits – *Gourmet Monthly*,' said Hisahiko casually, then took a sip of his tea. 'Publishers are all finding it hard to stay afloat these days, you see . . .'

'What kind of company is Tsuda Enterprises, anyway?' asked Koishi, eyeing his business card as she wiped the table down.

'Oh, we do everything. Finance, property, restaurants, publishing . . . If it's a viable business, we'll try it.'

'*C-E-O* . . . ?' said Koishi, picking up the business card.

'Chief Executive Officer. Basically what we call a kaicho

in Japanese,' said Hisahiko, taking another sip of his tea and tapping away at something on his phone.

'Quite young for one of those, aren't you!' said Koishi, her glance darting between the card and Hisahiko's face.

'Koishi, could you bring me some matcha?' said Tae, setting her chopsticks down on the table and turning in her chair to face her.

'Already?' asked Koishi, looking over. 'But you haven't finished your meal!'

'Oh, I'm not asking for a cup of tea, silly. I mean matcha powder.'

'Ah, wanting to mix it with your tempura salt, are you?' asked Nagare, emerging from the kitchen with a small porcelain bowl.

'I knew you'd figure it out, Nagare,' said Tae.

'I should have brought you some earlier,' said Nagare, setting the bowl of powdered matcha down alongside the black lacquer tray from which she was eating.

'Now, this may just be my imagination, but today's wild vegetable tempura seemed to lack that slight bitterness it should have.'

Tae mixed the matcha into the mound of salt by her dish, then pressed the koshiabura tempura into it and took a bite.

'There really is no pleasing you sometimes, is there? It's true: the vegetables are a bit lacking in bitterness and fragrance this time. Went and foraged for them myself, up in the Kuta mountains, but still . . .' Nagare folded his arms and cocked his head to one side.

'You source all your ingredients yourself, do you?' asked Hisahiko, setting his phone down on the table.

'It's just wild vegetables and mushrooms that I venture into the mountains for. They're always so much more flavourful than what you find at the markets,' said Nagare, briefly glancing in Hisahiko's direction.

'You really don't mess around in Kyoto, do you? I can't wait for the meal.'

'Just a moment,' said Nagare, hurrying off to the kitchen.

'I don't know where you're from, but don't go thinking every restaurant in Kyoto is like this. This place is *special*,' said Tae, fixing Hisahiko with a stern gaze.

'Oh, I'm just an uninformed Tokyoite. Though I was born in rural Hiroshima, actually, so deep down I'm a real country bumpkin!' said Hisahiko, smiling with one cheek only.

'Actually, if anything, Tokyo is where the real bumpkins are,' said Tae, turning her back on him. 'Not that a young person would understand that.'

'Sorry for the wait,' said Nagare, setting a large basket woven from green bamboo down on the table. 'I figured a youngster like you would have a hearty appetite. So I prepared extra.'

'Wow,' said Hisahiko, his eyes widening.

'Seeing as it's cherry season, I've gone for an imitation of a lunchbox from a blossom-viewing picnic. On top of that folded kaishi paper is the wild vegetable tempura. Ostrich fern, mugwort, devil's walking stick, koshiabura and smilax. There's some matcha salt on the side, or you can try it with the regular dipping sauce. The sashimi is cherry bass and halfbeak. Try it with the ponzu. For the grilled fish dish, I've gone with masu salmon in a miso marinade, together with some simmered young bamboo. Firefly squid and wakame seaweed dressed with vinegared miso, overnight Omi beef, and deep-fried chicken wing-tips. In that wooden bowl is an Asari clam and bamboo shoot broth. There's bamboo shoots in the rice too, but I can serve you some plain white rice if you'd prefer. There's more of everything, so just let me know if you'd like seconds. Well, tuck in!'

As Nagare spoke, Hisahiko's eyes darted left, right, up and down as he took in the array of dishes, nodding all the while.

'This is quite a feast! I don't even know where to start.'

Turning to face him again, Tae said, 'I should warn you—' but Hisahiko finished her sentence for her:

'I get it. Not every restaurant in Kyoto is like this – this place is special. Right?' He smiled at Tae, then began by reaching towards the Omi beef with his chopsticks.

'I see you've got the message.'

'Wow,' said Hisahiko, closing his eyes as he slowly savoured the rich umami of the meat. 'So tender. Really melts in your mouth.'

'That'll be because I stewed it for so long,' said Nagare, watching approvingly. 'Hope you enjoy the meal. When you're done, my daughter here will give you a brief interview about the dish you're looking for.'

'I'll leave the teapot here – just let me know if you'd like any more,' said Koishi, following Nagare into the kitchen.

Hisahiko reached for the bowl of broth, took a sip, and let out a sigh. Next he pressed a piece of wild vegetable tempura into the matcha salt and took a bite. The crunch was audible across the restaurant. Then he dipped the extra-thin slice of cherry bass sashimi in the ponzu and placed it on his tongue.

'Incredible flavour. I'm guessing the fish is from the Inland Sea . . .' said Hisahiko to himself, though he seemed to be waiting for Tae's reaction.

'The Uwa Bay, I believe,' murmured Tae without turning around.

'I see. No wonder it tastes so good,' said Hisahiko, his mouth now stuffed with bamboo shoot rice.

He must have been pretty hungry, because in no time at all, he had demolished each of the remaining dishes – the grilled fish, deep-fried chicken wing-tips, simmered bamboo, and the miso-dressed squid – leaving only the empty green bamboo basket.

'How was that, then?' asked Nagare, arriving at Hisahiko's side with a Mashiko-ware earthen teapot.

'Oh, exquisite,' replied Hisahiko, a smile spreading across his face. 'I mean, when a connoisseur like Akane raves about somewhere, you know you're in for a treat, but still . . .'

'Glad to hear it. Here – let me pour you some coarse green tea,' said Nagare, swapping the Kyo-ware teapot for the Mashiko one. When you've had a sip of that, give me a shout and I'll show you to the office.'

'Nagare, I'm ready for that mochi, if you could bring it over?' said Tae.

'Of course. I hope you like it wrapped in cherry leaves. I suppose you'd like your matcha tea nice and strong, as usual?'

'Well, if it's sakura-mochi you're serving me, it might be best to brew it a little weaker than usual.'

'Let me guess – because the mochi isn't actually that sweet?'

'Exactly.'

Once Nagare and Tae had finished their exchange, Hisahiko got to his feet, rubbing his stomach. 'Thank you for the food. I can make my own way to the office – I can see you're busy in here. Through that door on the left and straight down the corridor, is it? Akane told me all about it. I should be fine.'

'If you're sure. Koishi will be waiting for you in there!' said Nagare, gesturing towards the door.

'Oh, don't worry about me, Nagare,' said Tae. 'There's no rush – go ahead and show him the way!'

'I think I'm old enough to find my way down a corridor, thank you! Enjoy the rest of your meal.' Stifling a burp, Hisahiko opened the door at the back of the restaurant.

Pinned to the walls on either side of the long corridor was a vast array of photographs. A few were of people, but the majority were of food. In particular, Hisahiko found his gaze drawn towards those featuring meat dishes. He took a couple of paces, then stopped, before advancing and then stopping once more, repeating this procedure until eventually he found himself knocking on the door. A plate was fastened to it that read: *Kamogawa Detective Agency.*

'Please, come on in,' said Koishi, opening the door from inside as if she'd been waiting for this cue.

'Hello again,' said Hisahiko, sitting in the middle of the black sofa.

Koishi sat down opposite him, then placed a clipboard on the low table between them. 'Could you fill this out for me?'

'This is all very formal,' said Hisahiko, smiling with one cheek again as he gripped the pen.

'Well, you're here on Akane's recommendation, and we already have your card,' said Koishi guardedly. 'So I suppose you can just write your telephone number if you like.'

Without a moment's hesitation, Hisahiko scribbled away with his pen, and in less than a minute had handed the clipboard back to her.

'Hisahiko Tsuda. Thirty-three. Art Tower Residence, Roppongi Hills . . . Sounds like a pretty fancy place to live!' said Koishi with a sigh.

'Oh, I don't know about that. I host a lot of company events in the evenings, so it often feels more like an office. Though it's on the thirty-ninth floor, so at least the views are decent.'

'Thirty-ninth floor? We don't have anything that tall in Kyoto!'

'That's probably why the city still looks so beautiful,' said Hisahiko, glancing out of the window. 'I was born on a small island out in the sticks, so I find it easier to relax in places like this than Tokyo.'

'Which island was that, then?'

'Toyoshima. In the Inland Sea.' Hisahiko crossed his long legs.

'Whereabouts exactly?'

'You know Kure, near Hiroshima?'

'Yes, vaguely,' replied Koishi, imagining a map of the area in her head.

'Near there. There's a bridge linking it to the mainland now, but when I was growing up there you had to take a ferry.' A brooding look had come across Hisahiko's face.

'Is that where the dish you're looking for is from?' asked Koishi, cutting to the chase.

'Yes. It's the nikujaga stew I had when I was little,' said Hisahiko, leaning forward.

'What kind of nikujaga are we talking?' asked Koishi, jotting something down in her notebook.

'I don't remember,' said Hisahiko, his voice fading slightly. 'All I can tell you is that it was my mother who made it for me.'

'You don't remember at all?'

'No.'

'Oh dear. That doesn't give us much to go on. Can't you think of anything that might help?'

'My mother died from an illness when I was five, but just before that we moved from Toyoshima to a place called Kojima in Okayama prefecture. I can remember things pretty well after that, but those early years in Toyoshima are all a bit of a blur . . .'

'Your mother passed away twenty-eight years ago, then?' asked Koishi, still scribbling away.

'I have vague memories of playing with her, bath-time, exploring the island together, but I can't remember a thing about how her cooking tasted. All I know is that I loved it.'

'What did your parents do for a living?' asked Koishi, probing for some kind of clue.

'They ran a warehousing company. Dad was always boasting about how our family was the best off on the island. It's true that we lived comfortably – but then again, it was a pretty small island,' replied Hisahiko, his eyes downcast.

'Did they keep that up after you moved to Okayama?' asked Koishi, peering intently at Hisahiko.

'Yes, they took the company with them, but it went bust two years later. Later my father told me it was my mother's mounting medical costs that prevented them from properly investing in the business.'

'Was it a lengthy illness, then?'

'Five years she fought it. It turned out to be incurable.' Hisahiko's voice had dropped to a murmur.

'Must have been tough on your father, too.'

'Oh, he managed just fine. Actually, he got married again less than a year after she passed away. To the woman who looked after my mother at the hospital, no less.' A frosty smile had risen to Hisahiko's lips.

'I guess he thought a young child like you needed a mother figure.'

'But she was her carer! And then one day I was expected to call her my mother . . . Not to mention the fact that I'd suddenly gained a sister seven years my senior.'

'Could I get everyone's names?'

'My father was Hisanao, and my mother, Kimie. My stepmother's name is Sachiko. And Miho is my stepsister.' Hisahiko spoke in an entirely businesslike tone, watching Koishi's hand as she wrote.

'And what are they all up to these days?'

'My father died the spring I finished primary school,' continued Hisahiko, his gaze dropping to the low table in front of him. 'I spent the next six years of middle and high school living with my stepmother and her daughter. I was the interloper in their happy family, see? Oh, I hated it. As soon as I finished school, I ran away from home, swapping Okayama for Tokyo.'

'So you were eighteen when you left home. And it's been—' Koishi counted on her fingers '—fifteen years since then.'

'I've been so focused on getting ahead that they've flown by.'

Koishi stopped writing. 'So you've made it all the way from Okayama to Tokyo. You're a hugely successful businessman. Why the sudden desire for nikujaga?'

'Well, it has to do with an interview I've agreed to. Are you familiar with the women's magazine *Enchant*?'

'Oh, of course. Actually, I'm a bit of a fan,' said Koishi, leaning forward eagerly. 'It's practically written for thirty-somethings like me. Let me guess – they're featuring you in the *Men Who've Made It* section . . .'

'That's right. The interview is next month. They want to ask about all sorts. The secret to my success, my daily routine these days – and there's a part where I have to talk about a dish my mother used to make for me.'

'Oh yes,' said Koishi, scribbling away again. 'They always have that bit about men craving their mother's cooking.'

'So I asked myself if there was a dish like that, and the first thing that came to mind was her nikujaga stew.' Hisahiko's voice was tinged with sadness.

'Even though you couldn't remember what the stew was like, or how it tasted?' asked Koishi, a sceptical look on her face.

'All I knew was that if I ever had a comfort food, that was it,' said Hisahiko, pursing his lips.

'But . . . you don't remember it,' said Koishi, leaning back on the sofa.

'I do know that I liked it. And I have this vague sense that it was much redder than usual nikujaga, for some reason. That's about it, though. But there *is* another version of the stew that I do remember quite clearly,' said Hisahiko, furrowing his brow.

'Another version?' asked Koishi, leaning forward and grabbing her pen.

'It was the spring holidays just after I'd finished middle school. I'd gone to register at my new high school, and by the time I got home Sachiko had already made dinner. She'd gone out somewhere with Miho, and when I wandered into the kitchen I found two pots of nikujaga sitting there.'

'Two pots?' asked Koishi in an intrigued voice.

'I tried them both – and they tasted completely different,' said Hisahiko glumly. 'One of them was much tastier than the nikujaga I was used to. It was filled with cuts of beef. That was Sachiko and Miho's stew. Mine was the other one, which had no meat in it. But when she served it, there was some meat in there. I guess she lost her nerve and added it at the last minute . . .'

'I'm sure she just used two pots because it wouldn't all fit in one,' said Koishi, as if trying to console him.

'No,' said Hisahiko, pursing his lips again in displeasure. 'Even at that age, I could easily taste the difference. I was furious they'd been deceiving me like that . . . Treating me that way, just because I wasn't related to them by blood – can you imagine!'

'Oh, dear . . .' Koishi seemed a little lost for words.

'That was when I made my decision. I'd leave home and make my own fortune. And then, one day, I'd get my own back on those two . . .' Hisahiko was clenching his fists.

'Still, you don't remember a thing about the stew your mother used to make,' said Koishi, frowning. 'This is going to be a bit of a challenge.'

'I don't suppose this'll help much, but as I said, we lived quite comfortably on Toyoshima, so I reckon she used high-quality meat,' said Hisahiko, sitting up straight. 'All I can remember is my father saying, "Most people don't get to eat this kind of meat, son!"'

'But the seasoning is the most important part. If we don't know that, then it doesn't matter how good the meat was . . .' Koishi flicked through the pages of her notebook, a troubled expression on her face.

'There is one other thing . . .' said Hisahiko, hesitantly.

'What?' asked Koishi, looking intently at him.

'Well, for some reason, whenever I try to remember my mother's nikujaga, I think of mountains.'

'Mountains? Nikujaga and . . . mountains. Hmm . . .' said Koishi, folding her arms and gazing up at the ceiling.

Hisahiko seemed to gather himself slightly. 'I *was* only five, remember.'

'High-quality meat, and mountains. That's really not a

lot to go on if we're to try and recreate the dish . . .' sighed Koishi.

'If it really is hopeless, I do have a back-up,' said Hisahiko. There was something confrontational about his gaze.

'Back-up?'

'I'm thinking of going to Yoshimi Tateno – you know, the famous celebrity chef. You might have seen him on television? They call him the prince of modern Japanese cuisine. He's a friend of mine,' said Hisahiko proudly. 'I'm sure he'll know just how to use the finest ingredients in order to recreate that stew from my childhood.'

Though irritated, Koishi remained silent. Out of consideration for Nagare's feelings, she decided not to record this last piece of information in the notebook.

'And how are your mother and sister these days?'

'I went back to Kojima for my coming-of-age ceremony. That was the last time I set foot in that house.'

'So you haven't seen them in thirteen years.'

'Indeed. Nor do I feel any need to,' said Hisahiko disdainfully.

'Right then. Well, we'll do our best,' said Koishi, shutting her notebook.

'The interview is next month. If it turns out to be beyond

your abilities, please do let me know as soon as possible, and I can move on to my back-up,' said Hisahiko, rising to his feet.

Hisahiko was familiar with the building's layout by now. He strolled back down the corridor and opened the door to the restaurant.

'Finished already?' asked Nagare, hastily folding up the newspaper he'd been reading.

'Yes. Your daughter has all the details,' said Hisahiko, glancing over his shoulder at Koishi, who had followed him back into the restaurant.

'We'll recreate your dish as soon as possible,' said Nagare, getting to his feet and bowing.

'Let me know once you do,' said Hisahiko, returning the bow. 'I'll be here right away.'

'But aren't you a very busy man?'

'I've got plenty of talented people working for me. I might look busy, but I actually have all the time in the world,' grinned Hisahiko. 'I've been known to pitch up in Kyoto just for a bowl of black soy sauce ramen.'

'Well, I'll try not to let Akane down,' said Nagare, smiling back.

Koishi listened silently to this exchange between the two, then slid the door to the restaurant open.

'I'm counting on you!' said Hisahiko, making his way outside. As he did so, Drowsy came rushing over.

'Hey, you'll get his suit dirty!' said Koishi, scooping the tabby up in her arms.

Taking no notice of the cat, Hisahiko strolled off down Shomen-dori.

'Shouldn't you have talked to him a bit more?' said Koishi once they were back inside. 'This is definitely a tough one, Dad.' She gave Nagare a worried look.

'What's the dish?' asked Nagare, settling on one of the folding chairs.

'Nikujaga,' replied Koishi, sitting down opposite him.

'Ah, just as I thought. The way his mother used to cook it before she passed away, if I'm not mistaken?' said Nagare with a confident smile.

'How did you know?'

'See, Akane got in touch about a month ago with a request. Asked me to look into a man by the name of Hisahiko Tsuda. Wanted to know if he'd be a decent person to work for. So I've done some digging on him already, you see. Where he was born, what his childhood was like, what his work involves – that kind of thing.' Nagare got a folder out from the cupboard.

'So that sudden trip to Tokyo – that was to meet Akane, was it?' asked Koishi in a low voice.

'Couldn't leave her in the lurch, could I? She sounded desperate on the phone,' said Nagare, glancing through the folder.

'Dad?' said Koishi. Her expression was serious.

Nagare looked up at her. 'What?'

'. . . Oh, it's nothing.' Koishi glanced away, then got to her feet.

'You're a funny one,' said Nagare, still thumbing through the folder.

'Hey, Dad, remind me,' asked Koishi, changing the topic. 'What was Mum's nikujaga like?'

'Oh, just your regular stew, really. Chunks of beef, onions, carrots and konnyaku noodles. Irish Cobbler potatoes. Kikuko made the broth slightly sweeter than usual.' Nagare's hands had stopped moving, and a distant look had come over his face.

'Sounds just like your version!' smiled Koishi.

'I suppose it does.' Nagare shut the folder and turned his attention to the scribblings in Koishi's notebook.

'Mr Tsuda reckoned his mother used some kind of premium meat. Apparently they were quite wealthy in those days,' said Koishi, her nostrils flaring with distaste. 'I have to say, Dad, I'm not a huge fan of this guy.'

'Well, we've taken the job now. It doesn't matter whether

we like him,' replied Nagare firmly, his eyes still glued to the notebook.

'Oh, that's supposed to be a mountain, by the way,' said Koishi, pointing to a sketch in the corner of one page. It looked a little like Mount Fuji.

'A mountain? Hmm . . . Right, I think I'm off to Oka-yama,' said Nagare, unfolding a map.

'Okayama? But the stew is from when he lived on that island near Hiroshima!'

'Oh, I'll go there too. But the first port of call is definitely Okayama,' said Nagare, pointing to the city on the map.

'If you say so! Bring me back some kibi-dango dumplings, would you?' said Koishi, patting her father on the shoulder.

2

With the cherry blossoms at their peak, Kyoto was teeming with visitors. Knowing this would be the case, Hisahiko had reserved a taxi while still on the bullet train.

The black sedan was waiting for him at the eastern end of the Hachijo-dori exit from the station. He climbed in and told the driver the way to the Kamogawa Diner.

'You know,' said the driver, catching his eye in the rear-view mirror, 'I've been driving for thirty years and that's the first time I've heard of the place. Is it famous for a certain dish?'

'Well, it's nikujaga stew on the menu today,' replied Hisahiko, taking in the Kyoto scenery that was gliding past the window. 'Though I think they serve something different every day.'

The city's wide avenues and narrow alleys alike were crammed with vehicles. Hisahiko, frowning, glanced repeatedly at his watch.

When, over fifteen minutes after setting off, they finally arrived at the restaurant, Hisahiko was barely able to conceal his irritation.

'Keep the change. Just open the door, would you?'

The flustered driver operated the automatic door. Hisahiko sprang out and stood in front the Kamogawa Diner.

'We've been waiting for you!' said Koishi, sliding the door open.

'Thanks for inviting me back,' said Hisahiko, removing his beige spring coat as he walked into the restaurant.

'The traffic must have been pretty bad?' asked Nagare, smiling gently as he emerged from the kitchen.

'Yes, though I knew what I was in for,' shrugged Hisahiko. He was wearing a black shirt.

'Are you nice and hungry?'

'Considering how early it is, yes, I'm quite peckish,' said Hisahiko, giving his usual lopsided smile as he glanced at the clock on the wall. It was barely half past eleven.

'Seeing as it's nikujaga we're serving you, I thought I'd

go for a sort of cafeteria style. Having the white rice on the side should also help you really savour the taste, too. It'll be ready in just a minute!' Nagare's features tensed slightly as he made his way back into the kitchen.

Hisahiko sat down on one of the red chairs, then got his phone out from his bag.

'Take a look at this.' He turned his screen in Koishi's direction.

'What is that? French cuisine?' asked Koishi, squinting at the phone.

'It's the nikujaga from my childhood – as recreated by Yoshimi Tateno,' said Hisahiko, smiling with both cheeks for once.

Koishi's eyes widened.

'The meat is A5-grade Matsusaka beef, and the potatoes are Northern Rubies from Hokkaido. Both of the finest quality. The broth is flavoured with Shimousa soy sauce from Chiba and a type of high-grade refined Japanese sugar normally used to make desserts. Of course, my mother probably didn't use ingredients quite like those. But Mr Tateno was so kind as to suggest that, given how I've turned out, the nikujaga I ate must have been of at least *similar* quality.'

'So . . . he wrapped those purple potatoes . . . up in those thin slices of sirloin?' said Koishi, wrinkling her nose. 'I'm pretty sure that's not nikujaga.'

'Here we are!' said Nagare, bringing a lacquered tray over to the table.

'I intend to try your version before deciding which to use for the interview.'

Nagare waited for Hisahiko to put his phone back in his bag, then set the small tray down on the table.

'This is . . . my mother's cooking?' Hisahiko leaned over the tray and began inspecting it in minute detail.

The antique Imari-ware bowl was full to the brim with stew. Alongside it was a smaller bowl, decorated with lines traced in bright cobalt pigment and piled with white rice, a small Shigaraki dish bearing some pickled cabbage, and a Negoro lacquered wooden bowl from which rose an appetizing cloud of steam.

'This is nikujaga the way your mother made it. Koshihi-kari rice from Hiroshima. Cooked so that it's all soft and sticky. Apparently you liked it that way.'

'I did? But how did you . . .'

'Let's talk about that when you've finished. On the side you have extra-pickled Hiroshimana cabbage. And the miso soup is with a sea bream broth and poached egg. All your favourites, I believe. Please, enjoy!'

Nagare bowed and walked off, followed by Koishi.

Hisahiko began by giving the stew a good sniff. He nodded deeply, then picked up his chopsticks and inserted a piece of beef into his mouth. As soon as he began chewing, he cocked his head as if in confusion. He tried some potato and onion, and a smile rose on his right cheek. Then, as if changing his mind, he reached for another piece of meat, then gazed at it intently before stuffing it into his mouth. Again, a perplexed look came across his features.

Now he picked up the wooden bowl and sipped the miso soup. He let out a short sigh. He used his chopsticks to break up the poached egg, then took another sip. This time, it was his left cheek that smiled. He spread the Hiroshimana cabbage out slightly, then wrapped a piece around a mouthful of the white rice and inserted it into his mouth. Finally, his smile spread across both sides of his face.

Sitting up in his chair slightly, he took another piece of beef from the stew, placed it on top of his rice, then brought it to his mouth. When he had finished savouring the meal, Hisahiko set his chopsticks back down on the table.

'How was that, then? Bring back some memories?' asked Nagare, appearing with a Mashiko-ware teapot in his hand.

'The miso soup, the pickles and the rice were all very nostalgia-inducing, yes. But the stew itself isn't quite right, I'm afraid. Mr Kamogawa, this isn't the nikujaga that my mother made – it's the way Sachiko used to make it. You must have misunderstood me – I wanted you to recreate it the way my *real* mother made it, not my stepmother. And unfortunately, there won't be time for a second attempt. Of course, I'll pay you for your efforts. Please send an invoice to the address on my card.' Hisahiko rose from his seat and began gathering his things.

'Hang on a second . . .' said Koishi, flustered as she glanced between Hisahiko and Nagare.

'So you *do* remember, then,' declared Nagare, calmly. 'It's just as you say: this is the nikujaga that Sachiko used to make you.'

'But that's not what I asked for!' chuckled Hisahiko ironically as he pulled on his beige coat.

'Actually, I think you'll find it is,' said Nagare, looking Hisahiko right in the eye.

'What are you talking about?' said Hisahiko, his tone growing more abrupt. 'I requested my mother Kimie's stew. This was Sachiko's stew. Almost everything about it was different. There's simply no comparison!'

'Ah, but there is. In fact, it's the exact same dish.'

'How could it be?' said Hisahiko, turning red in the face. 'My mother and Sachiko were quite different people.'

'If you're in a rush, feel free to leave. It looks like you're not happy with the result, so there'll be no need to pay. But,' continued Nagare with a gentle smile, 'if you do have time to listen to what I have to tell you, please – take a seat.'

'Well, I'm not exactly in a rush . . .' said Hisahiko. He removed his coat and sat back down, a reluctant expression on his face.

'As you said, this is Sachiko's recipe. I got it from her. That's why there's none of that red colour you remembered. Apart from that, however, the taste should be identical. Sachiko is doing well, by the way. I paid a visit to that small house of hers, on the outskirts of Kojima.'

Nagare showed Hisahiko a photograph of a small, single-storey house with a red, corrugated roof.

'She's still . . . living there?' said Hisahiko in surprise as he took the photo.

'Miho got married seven years ago, and Sachiko has been there on her own ever since. Your room is still there too – just the way you left it.'

Hisahiko remained silent, seemingly unable to tear his eyes away from the photograph.

'Now, about this nikujaga. It turns out the recipe is one that your mother passed on to Sachiko. She wrote it in here,' said Nagare, placing a faded notebook on the table. 'What ingredients to use, how to flavour the broth – it's all there in detail. Sachiko was kind enough to let me borrow it.'

'*Cooking for Hisahiko*,' read Hisahiko, glancing at the title on the front page before hastily opening the notebook. 'My mother wrote this?'

'When your mother was in poor health, she knew she wouldn't be able to look after you for much longer. She asked Sachiko to take her place, as your father's second wife.

You were a fussy eater, so she decided to write down exactly what you liked.'

'And she gave Sachiko . . .' murmured Hisahiko, his eyes eagerly scanning the pages.

'Nikujaga is on the fifth page,' explained Nagare. Hisahiko hurriedly turned to the recipe.

'Kure, the district which the island of Toyoshima belongs to, is said to be the birthplace of nikujaga stew. Now, with Kure-style nikujaga you'd normally use May Queen potatoes, which don't fall apart when you boil them, but your mother Kimie used a famous brand of potato from Akasaki, not far from the island. Dejima potatoes, they're called – and still popular to this day. The onions were from Awajima, and the soy sauce from Shodoshima. This was almost thirty years ago, so sourcing ingredients of that quality would have been quite a challenge. You must really have been the apple of her eye.'

'But what about here, where it says "Yamato-ni"?' asked Hisahiko, his eyes glued to the notebook. 'Does that mean she used . . .'

'That's right. Canned meat,' said Nagare, placing a can on the table. 'Yamato-ni – soy-stewed beef. Like it says in the notebook, in those days there was nowhere on the island that had a regular supply of high-quality beef. You weren't a fan of meat with a lot of fat on it, which was why your mother used the canned stuff, which was reliably lean. And, seeing as she and your father ran a warehousing business, she probably had ways of getting her hands on it.

'The word "yamato-ni" must have come up in your parents' conversations,' continued Nagare, pointing at the characters emblazoned on the can. And, seeing as *yama* can also mean "mountain", I reckon you assumed that was what they were talking about. A kid your age would have known no better.'

'That explains that, then,' said Hisahiko, his eyes widening as he picked up the can and inspected it.

'The reason you remembered the stew having a reddish tinge is because when you were little you didn't like carrots, and so your mother would mash them up before they went in the stew. But by the time Sachiko took over, you no longer minded them, so she started just chopping them up instead. Hence the difference in colour. Now, as for that time you found two pots on the stove. The reason one of them didn't have any meat in it was because Sachiko was using the canned stuff for you. It's already cooked and seasoned, so she would have just popped it in when the stew was ready to serve. As she must have realized, it's so lean that if you boil it too long it turns all tough.'

'These days, you're more likely to find me eating a cut of marbled beef,' said Hisahiko.

'The fat on a quality cut of meat is delicious, but less so on something cheaper. Your tastes might have changed as you got older, but Sachiko followed your mother's recipe to the letter. She's a very conscientious woman.'

Nagare showed him a photo of Sachiko standing in front of her house.

'She's so small now,' said Hisahiko, his eyes glistening slightly.

'The recipes for the pickled cabbage and poached-egg miso soup are written in different handwriting, so they can't have been your mother's. I reckon Sachiko wrote those down herself,' said Nagare, pouring Hisahiko some more tea.

'I never even knew this existed,' said Hisahiko, shutting the notebook and gently stroking its cover.

'You only ever ate one type of nikujaga stew, Hisahiko. One mother simply handed the baton over to another.'

'So Sachiko went to the trouble of making a separate stew, just for me . . .' murmured Hisahiko, gazing into space as he remembered the two pots on the stove.

'Still, I imagine that whatever that celebrity chef cooked up for you will make much better content for a trendy women's magazine. I caught a glimpse of it just now, and it's certainly a good fit for your image. Canned meat would come across a little rustic, wouldn't it?'

Hisahiko remained silent, still running a finger across the notebook.

'Sachiko is very proud that you've made such a name for

yourself, by the way. She's got this scrapbook full of cut-
tings from articles about you. Very grateful for that sizeable
allowance you send her every New Year, too. Though she
hasn't touched a single yen of it.'

'I was hoping she'd use it to rebuild her house,' said
Hisahiko with a faint smile. 'Or buy a new one.'

'She's delighted that you've reached such dazzling
heights. But she's also worried you might come tumbling
down again one day,' explained Nagare in an almost admonishing tone. 'On the off-chance that happens, she wants to
be able to give you the money back. It doesn't matter that
she's not connected to you by blood – she's always planning
for her child's future. That's what parents do.'

'Thank you for everything.' Hisahiko turned to Koishi.
'So, how much do I owe you for this, plus the meal last
time?'

'Just send whatever you feel is right to this account,
please,' said Koishi, handing over a slip of paper with the
relevant details.

'Can I take the notebook and canned meat with me?'
Hisahiko asked Nagare.

'Of course,' said Nagare, looking Hisahiko in the eye.
'I've got five cans of the stuff here. I hope they won't weigh
you down too much.'

'Let me get you a paper bag,' said Koishi, opening a
cupboard.

'Don't worry – I'll just put them in here,' said Hisahiko, immediately tucking them into his pouch, which he hugged to his chest.

'I'll be looking forward to that issue of *Enchant*!' said Koishi as she slid open the door to the restaurant.

'I'll be sure to send you a copy when it's out.' As Hisahiko uttered his reply, Drowsy came padding over to where he stood.

'Cats really do have it easy, don't they? What's its name?' asked Hisahiko, stooping to stroke the animal.

'Drowsy. Always snoozing away, you see.' Koishi squatted down next to him, and the cat gave a single *miaow*.

'Give Akane my regards,' said Nagare as Hisahiko rose to his feet.

'Sorry, but I can't help asking,' said Hisahiko, turning to face Nagare. 'How do *you* know Akane?'

'She was friends with my wife before she passed away. My wife had known her since before we got married. She's like a little sister to me.'

'That explains the advert in *Gourmet Monthly*, then,' said Hisahiko, with a satisfied nod.

'It's a real food magazine, that,' said Nagare, pursing his lips. 'Not just some lightweight listings job. I reckoned that if we advertised in there, we'd be sure to get some decent clients – and anyone who did manage to find us would be worth knowing.'

'Please, if you're buying *Gourmet Monthly*, promise you'll look after it. And Akane too,' said Koishi.

Hisahiko bowed back, then set off west down the street. Nagare bowed in the direction of his departing figure, and Koishi followed suit.

'So, which nikujaga do you think he'll choose?' asked Koishi once they were back inside.

'I'm not sure it matters,' replied Nagare casually.

'See how he stroked Drowsy this time?' said Koishi, folding her arms. 'Last time he didn't even seem to notice him. He must be in quite a different frame of mind.'

'Becoming something of a detective yourself, eh?'

'So you noticed it too?'

'Of course. Anyway, how about a night-time picnic under the cherry blossoms later? We can make a bento box for the occasion.'

'Brilliant idea, Dad. Let's take plenty to drink, too. Where would be good?'

'You know the Nakaragi path along the Kamogawa river? I hear the weeping cherries along there are looking spectacular. We can take the subway to Kita-Oji.'

'Don't you think Mum'll feel left out?' said Koishi, looking over at the altar.

'We'll just have to make enough for the three of us, and take her photo with us,' said Nagare, walking into the kitchen.

'Oh. There's something else we should take,' said Koishi, rushing into the living room and opening the chest of drawers.

'What's that?' said Nagare, peering over her shoulder.

'This,' said Koishi, clutching a pale pink stole to her chest. 'She always wore it. It's dyed with cherry blossom. Remember it?'

'Of course I do. I bought her it when we went to Shinshu on holiday, but then we left it on the train home. Kikuko was so devastated that she burst into tears. And then we managed to get it back, and she was so relieved that she started crying all over again . . .' Nagare's own eyes had begun to glisten.

'You know what, Dad?' said Koishi, tears trickling down her cheeks as she hugged the stole. 'I think one mum is plenty for me.'

Nagare smiled. 'You're more like her every day.'

The Kamogawa food detectives
will return in . . .

THE RESTAURANT
OF LOST RECIPES

Moving and uplifting, *The Restaurant of
Lost Recipes* features more heartwarming tales from
Kyoto's one-of-a-kind dining establishment.

PRE-ORDER NOW